Orkney &
Shetland

Alan Murphy

Credits

Footprint credits

Editor: Sophie Blacksell Jones
Production and layout: Emma Bryers
Maps: Kevin Feeney
Cover: Angus Dawson

Publisher: Patrick Dawson
Managing Editor: Felicity Laughton
Advertising: Elizabeth Taylor
Sales and marketing: Kirsty Holmes

Photography credits
Front cover: John Braid / Shutterstock.com
Back cover: John Braid / Dreamstime.com

Printed in Great Britain by alphaset, Surbition

Every effort has been made to ensure that the facts in this guidebook are accurate. However, travellers should still obtain advice from consulates, airlines, etc, about travel and visa requirements before travelling. The authors and publishers cannot accept responsibility for any loss, injury or inconvenience however caused.

The content of Footprint *Focus Orkney & Shetland* has been taken directly from Footprint's *Scotland Highlands & Islands Handbook*, which was researched and written by Alan Murphy.

Publishing information

Footprint *Focus Orkney & Shetland*
2nd edition
© Footprint Handbooks Ltd
April 2014

ISBN: 978 1 909268 83 8
CIP DATA: A catalogue record for this book is available from the British Library

® Footprint Handbooks and the Footprint mark are a registered trademark of Footprint Handbooks Ltd

Published by Footprint
6 Riverside Court
Lower Bristol Road
Bath BA2 3DZ, UK
T +44 (0)1225 469141
F +44 (0)1225 469461
footprinttravelguides.com

Distributed in the USA by Globe Pequot Press, Guilford, Connecticut

Contents

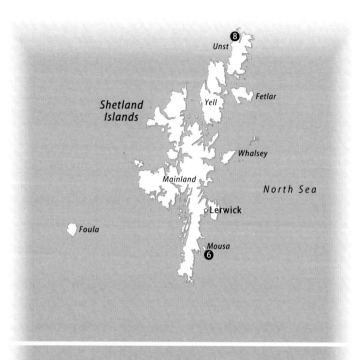

Shetland Islands

Unst

Yell

Fetlar

Whalsey

Mainland

North Sea

Lerwick

Mousa

Foula

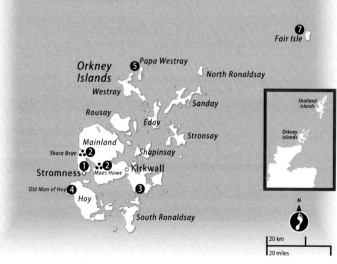

Fair Isle

Orkney Islands

Papa Westray

North Ronaldsay

Westray

Rousay

Sanday

Eday

Stronsay

Mainland

Shapinsay

Skara Brae

Stromness

Maes Howe

Kirkwall

Old Man of Hoy

Hoy

South Ronaldsay

Shetland Islands

Orkney Islands

N

20 km

20 miles

To some, these two archipelagos will never be anything other than distant and overlooked specks of land peppering the wild North Atlantic, above an already distant north coast of mainland Scotland. They certainly are remote and they have maintained a social and political, as well as geographical, distance from the rest of Scotland, which goes a long way to explaining the relatively few visitors each year. Both were under Norse rule until the mid-15th century and, somehow, seeing them as a part of Scotland can be very misleading. Each must be seen within the context of its own unique cultural background and unusual geography.

Shetland's northern islands, on the same latitude as Alaska, are as strange and different as Britain gets, while beguiling Orkney just smiles serenely as the rest of world races headlong into the future at alarming speed. It is these qualities that make the islands worth visiting and the ones that the tourist boards are keen to plug. Both Orkney and Shetland are littered with outstanding archaeological evidence, not just of six centuries of Norse occupation, such as at Jarlshof at the very southern tip of Shetland, but also of life back in 3000 BC at Skara Brae and the Knap of Howar in the Orkneys. They are also among the best places in Britain to see wildlife as yet untamed by the 21st century. Here you can sail alongside porpoises and seals, potentially spot killer whales (orca) and watch a million migratory seabirds nest and raise their young during the summer months. And, thanks to fast and frequent transport links, it doesn't take an Arctic expedition to get here.

Planning your trip

Best time to visit Orkney and Shetland

The high season is from May to September, and this is when the islands receive most of their visitors, although, even at this time of year, tourist numbers are limited. The weather tends to be better during the summer months and there are long hours of daylight; in Shetland the sun barely sets at all in June and July. Conversely, in mid winter it is dark most of the time and the weather can be bitter. Winter storms also make it difficult to travel between the islands as ferry services are often cancelled. From October to Easter, many sights, tourist offices and accommodation options are closed, and public transport services are limited. Whenever you travel, hotels and guesthouses should be booked in advance, and it's also a good idea to make reservations on ferries.

What to do in Orkney and Shetland

Blessed with wild landscapes and miles of remote coastline, Orkney and Shetland are paradise for the visitor who comes to unwind or in search of adventure amidst breathtaking scenery. They are also among the best places in Europe to see wildlife, especially marine birds and mammals, in an unspoilt setting. Furthermore, their unique history has bequeathed Orkney and Shetland some fascinating archaeological sites, evidence of over 5000 years of human habitation.

Birdwatching

① **Royal Society for the Protection of Birds**, 12-14 North End Rd, Stromness, KW16 3AG, T01856-850176 (in Orkney), T01950-460800 (in Shetland), www.rspb.org.uk, manages 13 reserves in Orkney and four in Shetland.

Orkney and Shetland are famous for their rich variety of birdlife and are home to large colonies of seabirds and migratory birds. There are puffins, kittiwakes, fulmars, shags, razorbills, guillemots and even auks. A more unusual and rare resident of Shetland is the snowy owl.

Cycling

① **Cyclists' Touring Club** (**CTC**), Parklands, Railton Rd, Guilford, Surrey, T0131-448 0930 (Scotland), www.ctc.org.uk, is the largest cycling organization in the UK. **Cycle Shetland**, T01595-989898, www.cycleshetland.com. **SUSTRANS**, T0845-113 0065, www.sustrans. org.uk, is the UK's leading sustainable transport charity. **VisitScotland**, www.visitscotland. com, for maps and details of cycle routes. It also publishes Cycling in Scotland (free), listing bike repair shops and operators.

Cycling is a good way to experience Orkney and Shetland: roads are nearly traffic free, there are wonderful landscapes all around and many of the islands are fairly flat, though most places are very exposed and the winds can be relentless and punishing. Bikes travel free on inter-island ferries in Orkney and on many services in Shetland. Ferries from mainland Scotland transport bikes for a small fee and airlines will often accept them as part of your baggage allowance. Check with the ferry company or airline about any restrictions.

Don't miss...

Diving

ⓘ **Sub Aqua**, www.subaqua.co.uk, has a list of dive operators. Scapa Flow in Orkney is world-renowned as the burial site of the German First World War fleet. Visibility is good and there is plenty of wildlife. Most dive operators are based in Stromness. There is also good diving off North Mainland in Shetland.

Fishing

ⓘ **Scottish Federation of Sea Anglers**, T01573-470612, www.fishsea.co.uk, provides comprehensive information on the main species to fish for and advice on where to fish. See also **www.visitscotland.com/fish** and **www.fishscotland.co.uk**, for a complete listing and key information about locations in Scotland

The islands' rivers, streams, lochs and estuaries are among the cleanest waters in Europe. Not surprisingly, fishing (coarse, game and sea) is hugely popular. For wild brown trout the close season is early October to mid-March. No licence is required to fish, but you must obtain a permit from the land owners or their agents. These are often readily available and usually cost from around £15.

Golf

ⓘ **VisitScotland**, www.visitscotland.com, provides a *Golfing in Scotland* brochure which gives a comprehensive break-down of prices and courses across the country, plus lists of accommodation providers. To arrange golfing holidays, visit **www.scotland-golf-tours.co.uk**.

The most northerly golf course in the UK can be found at Burra Firth on Unst in Shetland.

Walking

ⓘ For detailed information and routes, consult **www.walkhighlands.com**, **www.visit scotland.com**, **www.orkney.com/walking**, **www.walkshetland.com**.

Orkney and Shetland are great for walking. Throughout the islands there are numerous routes, ranging from short walks to long-distance treks. Whatever your taste or level of fitness and experience, you'll find plenty of opportunities to get off the beaten track and explore the countryside. Particularly good areas include the coasts of Westside and North Mainland in Shetland, plus the islands of Yell and Fetlar, and Hoy in Orkney.

Getting to Orkney and Shetland

Air

Generally speaking, the cheapest and quickest way to travel to Scotland from outside the UK is by air. There are good links to **Edinburgh** and **Glasgow**, with direct flights from many European cities, and direct flights from North America to Glasgow. There are also flights from a few European cities to **Aberdeen** and **Inverness**. There are also daily flights from Ireland and regular flights to most Scottish airports from other parts of the UK. There are no direct flights to Scotland from Australia, New Zealand, South Africa or Japan; you will have to get a connection from London. The only direct international route to Orkney and Shetland is from Bergen in Norway to **Kirkwall** or **Sumburgh**. All other international visitors must fly via a mainland UK airport.

From the UK and Ireland There are direct flights to Scotland's four main airports – Glasgow, Edinburgh, Aberdeen and Inverness – almost hourly from London Heathrow, Gatwick, Stansted and Luton airports. There are also daily flights from provincial UK airports and from Dublin. To fly on to the smaller airports, you'll need to change planes. The cheapest flights leave from London Luton or Stansted, plus a few provincial airports, with **Ryanair** and **easyJet**. If you book online, fares can be as little as £15 one-way during low season (excluding taxes), and you can expect to fly for around £70-100 return if you can be flexible with dates and times. These tickets are often subject to rigid restrictions, but the savings can make the extra effort worthwhile. Cheaper tickets usually have to be bought at least a month in advance (or much further in advance around school holidays) and apply to only a few midweek flights. They are also non-refundable, or only partly refundable, and non-transferable. A standard flexible and refundable fare from London to Glasgow or Edinburgh will cost at least £150-200 return. The flight from London to Glasgow and Edinburgh is roughly one hour.

Once you're in Scotland there are flights from Glasgow, Edinburgh and Inverness to **Kirkwall** (Orkney) and **Sumburgh** (Shetland) with **Flybe** franchise partner, **Loganair** (www.flybe.com or www.loganair.co.uk). Internal flights are relatively expensive, however. For example a return flight from Edinburgh or Glasgow to Shetland can cost over £200. There are discounted tickets available, which must be booked at least 14 days in advance, and special offers on some services. There is no departure tax on flights from Highlands and Islands airports. For full details of all flights to Highlands and Islands airports from the rest of the UK, visit the **Highlands and Islands Airports Ltd** website, www.hial.co.uk.

From the rest of Europe There are direct flights to **Glasgow International** from many European capitals, including Copenhagen, Amsterdam, Paris (Beauvais), Dublin, Frankfurt, Stockholm, Brussels, Milan, Oslo and Barcelona. There are flights to **Edinburgh** from Paris (CDG), Zurich, Amsterdam, Brussels, Copenhagen and Frankfurt; direct flights to **Aberdeen** from Amsterdam, Copenhagen and Stavanger; and to **Inverness** from Amsterdam and Zurich.

From North America Because of the much larger number of flights to London, it is generally cheaper to fly there first and get an onward flight, see above for the best deals. East Coast USA to Glasgow takes around six to seven hours direct. To London it takes seven hours. From the West Coast it takes an additional four hours. **Continental Airlines** and **KLM** fly from New York to Glasgow International, **Aer Lingus** and **KLM** fly from Chicago and **Air Canada** from Toronto.

Airport information Glasgow International ① *T0844-481 5555, www.glasgowairport. com*, is eight miles west of the city, at junction 28 on the M8. It handles domestic and international flights. Terminal facilities include car hire, bank ATMs, currency exchange, left luggage, tourist information, and shops, restaurants and bars. **Edinburgh airport** ① *T0844-448 8833, www.edinburghairport.com*, has all facilities, including a tourist information desk, currency exchange, ATMs, restaurants and bars (first floor), shops (ground floor and first floor) and car hire desks in the terminal in the main UK arrivals area. For details of facilities and amenties at all Highlands and Islands airports, visit www.hial.co.uk.

Rail

The rail network in Scotland is limited and train travel is comparatively expensive, but trains are a fast and effective way to get around and also provide some beautifully scenic journeys. **ScotRail** operates most train services within Scotland. You can buy train tickets at the stations, from major travel agents, or over the phone with a credit or debit card. For information and advance credit or debit card bookings visit www.scotrail.co.uk. For busy long-distance routes it's best to reserve a seat. Seat reservations to Edinburgh, Glasgow, Aberdeen or Inverness are included in the price of the ticket when you book in advance. Cycles are carried free of charge on **ScotRail** services, although reservations are required on longer distance routes.

Eurorail passes are not recognized in Britain, but ScotRail offers a couple of worthwhile rail passes. The most flexible is the *Freedom of Scotland Travelpass*, which gives unlimited rail travel within Scotland. It is also valid on **CalMac** ferries, many **Citylinkbus** services, some regional buses and offers discounts on some city centre bus tours. It also gives 20% discount on **Northlink Ferries** between Scrabster–Stromness, Aberdeen–Lerwick and Aberdeen–Kirkwall–Lerwick. It costs £134 for four days' travel out of eight consecutive days, £179 for eight out of 15.

There are fast and frequent rail services from London and other main towns and cities in England to Glasgow, Edinburgh, Aberdeen and Inverness. Journey time from London is about 4½ hours to Edinburgh, five hours to Glasgow, seven hours to Aberdeen and eight hours to Inverness. Two companies operate direct services from London to Scotland: **National Express** trains (www.east coast.co.uk) leave from King's Cross and run up the east coast to Edinburgh, Aberdeen and Inverness, and **Virgin** trains leave from Euston and run up the west coast to Glasgow. **ScotRail** operate the *Caledonian Sleeper* service if you wish to travel overnight from London Euston or Northwest England to Aberdeen, Edinburgh, Glasgow, Inverness and Fort William. This runs nightly from Sunday to Friday. There are numerous fare options. For more information, see www.scotrail.co.uk or the excellent www.seat61.com.

Eurostar ① *T08705-186186 (+44-123-361 7575), www.eurostar.com*, operates high-speed trains through the Channel Tunnel to London St Pancras International from Paris (2½ hours), Brussels (two hours) and Lille (1½ hours). You then have to change trains, and stations, for the onward journey north to Scotland. If you're driving from continental Europe you could take *Le Shuttle*, which runs 24 hours a day, 365 days a year, and takes you and your car from Calais to Folkestone in 35 to 45 minutes. Depending on how far in advance you book, or when you travel, cheaper fares are available, call T08705-353535 for bookings.

Enquiries and booking National Rail Enquiries ① *T08457-484950, www.nationalrail. co.uk*, are quick and courteous with information on rail services and fares but not always accurate, so double check. They can't book tickets but will provide you with the relevant telephone number. The website, www.qjump.co.uk, is a bit hit-and-miss but generally fast and efficient, and shows you all the various options on any selected journey, while www.thetrainline.co.uk, also has its idiosyncrasies but shows prices clearly. For advance card bookings, contact **National Express**, www.nationalexpress; **ScotRail**, www.scotrail.co.uk; and **Virgin**, www.virgintrains.co.uk.

Fares   To describe the system of rail ticket pricing as complicated is a huge understatement and impossible to explain here. There are many and various discounted fares, but restrictions are often prohibitive, which explains the long queues and delays at ticket counters in railway stations. The cheapest ticket is an Advance ticket or Value Advance (Virgin), which must be booked in advance (obviously), though this is not available on all journeys. A GNER London–Edinburgh Advance Single costs between around £25 and £100. Advance Singles with ScotRail on this route start from around £50 for direct trains. All discount tickets should be booked as quickly as possible as they are often sold out weeks, or even months, in advance. A Caledonian Sleeper 'Bargain Berth' single ticket from London to Edinburgh or Glasgow costs from around £25-30; to book visit www.scotrail.co.uk.

Railcards   There are a variety of railcards which give discounts on fares for certain groups. Cards are valid for one year and most are available from main stations. You need two passport photos and proof of age or status.

Disabled Person's Railcard   Costs £20 for one year and gives 33% discount to a disabled person and one other. Pick up an application form from stations and send it to Disabled Person's Railcard Office, PO Box 163, Newcastle-upon-Tyne, NE12 8WX. It may take up to 21 days to process, so apply in advance (www.disabledpersons-railcard.co.uk).

Family & Friends Railcard   Costs £30 and gives 33% discount on most tickets for up to four adults travelling together, and 60% discount for up to four children.

Senior Citizen's Railcard   For those aged over 60. Same price and discounts as above (www.senior-railcard.co.uk).

Young Person's Railcard   For those aged 16-25 or full-time students aged 26+ in the UK. Costs £30 for one year and gives 33% discount on most train tickets and some other services (www.16-25railcard.co.uk).

Road
Bus/coach   Road links to Scotland are excellent, and a number of companies offer express coach services day and night. This is the cheapest form of travel to Scotland but may not be practical if you're travelling up to Orkney and Shetland due to the huge distances and long journey times. The main operator between England and Scotland is **National Express** ① T08717-818178, www.nationalexpress.com. There are direct buses from most British cities to Edinburgh, Glasgow, Aberdeen and Inverness. Tickets can be bought at bus stations or from a huge number of agents throughout the country. Fares from London to Glasgow and Edinburgh with **National Express** start at around £30 return (online discount fare). Fares to Aberdeen and Inverness are a little higher. The London to Glasgow/Edinburgh journey takes around eight hours, while it takes around 11 to 12 hours for the trip to Aberdeen and Inverness. From Manchester to Glasgow takes around 6½ hours.

Travelling around Scotland by bus takes longer than the train but is much cheaper. There are numerous local bus companies, but the main operator is **Scottish Citylink** ① www.citylink.co.uk. Bus services between towns and cities are good, but far less frequent in more remote rural areas. There are a number of discount and flexible tickets available and details of these are given on the **Citylink** website, which is fast and easy to use. **John o'Groats** ferries run the **Orkney Bus** from Inverness to Kirkwall via John o'Groats (see page 61).

Car There are two main routes to Scotland from the south. In the east the A1 runs to Edinburgh and in the west the M6 and A74(M) runs to Glasgow. The journey north from London to either city takes around eight to 10 hours. The A74(M) route to Glasgow is dual carriageway all the way. A slower and more scenic route is to head off the A1 and take the A68 through the Borders to Edinburgh. If you have time, then travelling with your own private transport is a great way to see Scotland en route to Orkney and Shetland. The main disadvantage is the rising fuel costs (around £1.40 per litre for diesel). Roads in the Highlands and Islands are a lot less busy than those in England, and driving is relatively stress-free, especially on the B-roads and minor roads. You should pre-book car-ferry crossings to the islands (see Sea, page 12).

To drive in Scotland you must have a current **driving licence**. Foreign nationals also need an international **driving permit**, available from state and national motoring organizations for a small fee. Those importing their own vehicle should also have their vehicle registration or ownership document. Make sure you're adequately **insured**. In all of the UK you drive on the left. **Speed limits** are 30 miles per hour (mph) in built-up areas, 70 mph on motorways and dual carriageways, and 60 mph on most other roads.

It's advisable to join one of the main UK motoring organizations during your visit for their 24-hour breakdown assistance. The two main ones in Britain are the **Automobile Association (AA)** ① *T0800-085 2721, www.theaa.com*, and the **Royal Automobile Club (RAC)** ① *T08705-722722, www.rac.co.uk*. One year's membership of the AA starts at £32 and £30 for the RAC. They also provide many other services, including a reciprocal agreement for free assistance with many overseas motoring organizations. Check to see if your organization is included. Both companies can also extend their cover to include Europe. Their emergency numbers are: **AA**, T0800-887766; **RAC**, T0800-828282. You can call these numbers even if you're not a member, but you'll have to a pay a large fee. In remote areas you may have to wait a long time for assistance. Also note that in the Highlands and Islands you may be stranded for ages waiting for spare parts to arrive.

If you fly into Scotland, car hire is available at the airports and need not be expensive if you shop around for the best deals. **AVIS** (see below) offers weekend rates from around £50 and £130 for the week, though whichever operator you choose be wary of high charges for additional mileage. Even without deals you should be able to hire a small car for a week from £150. Local hire companies often offer better deals than the larger multi-nationals, though **easyCar** can offer the best rates, at around £10 per day, if you book in advance and don't push up the charges with high mileage. They are based at Aberdeen, Glasgow, Edinburgh and Inverness airport. Many companies such as **Europcar** offer the flexibility of picking up in Glasgow and leaving in Edinburgh, and vice versa. Most companies prefer payment with a credit card, otherwise you'll have to leave a large deposit (£100 or more). You'll need a full driver's licence (one or two years) and be aged over 21 (23 in some cases).

Alternatively, why not hire your own transport and accommodation at the same time by renting a campervan. Campervans can be rented from a number of companies and it's best to arrange this before arriving as everything gets booked up in the high season (June-August). Inverness-based **Highland Camper Vans,** www.highlandcampervans.com, is a good bet with a range of vans starting at £120 per day/night for its four-person touring van.

Sea

You can travel to Scotland by sea from Ireland. **P&O Irish Sea** ① *T0871-664 2020, www. poferries.com*, has several crossings daily from Larne to Cairnryan (one hour), and from Larne to Troon (two hours). Fares are from £74 each way for car and driver. **Stena Line** ① *T0870-570 7070, www.stenaline.co.uk*, runs numerous ferries (three hours) and high-speed catamarans (1½ hours) from Belfast to Stranraer, fares from £69 single for car and driver.

Northlink Ferries ① *T0845-6000 449, www.northlinkferries.co.uk*, run car ferries to Orkney and Shetland. Ferries to Orkney depart from Aberdeen or from Scrabster, near Thurso. There are also car and passenger ferries to Orkney with **Pentland Ferries** ① *www. pentlandferries.co.uk*, and a passenger-only ferry (summer only) with **John o'Groats Ferries** ① *www.jogferry.co.uk*. See pages 32 and 60 for full details of these. Ferries to Shetland sail from Aberdeen. See page 63.

Transport in Orkney and Shetland

Getting around these remote destinations without your own transport requires careful planning and an intimate knowledge of rural bus timetables. Hiring a car can work out as a more economical and certainly more flexible option, especially for more than two people travelling together. It will also enable you to get off the beaten track and see more. Even if you're driving, however, getting around the remote islands can be a time-consuming business. Be sure to refuel regularly, allow plenty of time and book ferries in advance.

Air

Loganair ① *T01856-886210, www.loganair.co.uk*, operates flights between Kirkwall and Sumburgh (Shetland) as well as inter-island flights around Orkney (see page 32). **Directflight** ① *T01595-840246, www.directflight.co.uk*, operates inter-island services in Shetland from Tingwall airport near Lerwick (see page 65).

Road

Bus Public transport in Orkney is limited to the major settlements on Mainland. Shetland, however, has a comprehensive bus network on Mainland, with links from Lerwick to most destinations around the island. Unst, Fetlar and Bressay have limited post bus services.

Car and campervan Travelling with your own private transport is the ideal way to explore Orkney and Shetland. This allows you to cover a lot of ground in a short space of time and to reach remote places. Roads have very light traffic and driving is relatively stress-free. Many roads are single track, with passing places indicated by a diamond-shaped signpost. These should also be used to allow traffic behind you to overtake. Remember that you may want to take your time to enjoy the stupendous views all around you, but the driver behind may be a local doctor in a hurry. Don't park in passing places. A major driving hazard on single track roads are the huge number of sheep wandering around, blissfully unaware of your presence. When confronted by a flock of sheep, slow down and gently edge your way past. Be particularly careful at night, as many of them sleep by the side of the road (counting cars perhaps). Car hire is available in Kirkwall, Stomness and Stronsay, Orkney, and in Lerwick and at Sumburgh airport, Shetland.

Hitching The Orkney and Shetland islands may be among the safest places in the UK to hitch a ride but, even so, hitching is never without risk and is certainly not advised for anyone travelling alone, particularly women travellers. You should not find it too difficult to get a lift in Orkney and Shetland, where people are far more willing to stop for you. Bear in mind, though, that you will probably have to wait a while even to see a vehicle in some parts.

Sea

The Orkney Islands are linked by services run by **Orkney Ferries** ① *www.orkney ferries. co.uk*, while Shetland's heavily subsidized inter-island ferries are run by **Shetland Islands Council** ① *www.shetland.gov.uk*. There are also numerous small operators offering day-trips to various islands. For details of these services, see pages 33 and 65.

Most ferries carry vehicles and can be booked in advance. If you're travelling to the islands by car, it's a good idea to book ferries in advance whatever the time of year, particularly to the more popular islands.

Maps

You'll find a good selection of maps of Scotland in many bookshops and at the main tourist offices. Road atlases can be bought at most service stations. The best of these are the large-format ones produced by the **AA**, **Collins** and **Ordnance Survey**, which cover all of Britain at a scale of around three miles to one inch and include plans of the major towns and cities. The **Michelin** and **Bartholomew** fold-out maps are also excellent, as are the official regional tourist maps published by **Estate Publications**, which are ideal for driving and are available from most tourist offices.

The best detailed maps for walking are the Ordnance Survey (OS) maps, which are unsurpassed for accuracy and clarity. These are available at different scales. The Landranger series at 1:50,000 (1¼ inches to a mile) covers the whole of Britain and is good for most walkers. The new Explorer and Outdoor Leisure series are 1:25,000 and offer better value for walkers and cyclists. An excellent source of maps is **Stanfords** ① *12-14 Longacre, London, T020-7836 1321, www.stanfords.co.uk*. There are branches of Stanfords in Bristol and Manchester too.

Where to stay in Orkney and Shetland

Staying in Orkney and Shetland can mean anything from living the high life in a mansion to roughing it in a tiny island böd with no electricity. There are many good-value small hotels and guesthouses. At the bottom end of the scale, there are also some excellent hostels in some pretty special locations.

We have tried to give as broad a selection as possible to cater for all tastes and budgets but if you can't find what you're after, or if someone else has beaten you to the draw, then the tourist information centres (TICs) will help find accommodation for you. They can recommend a place within your particular budget and give you the number to phone up and book yourself, or will book a room for you. Some offices charge a small fee (usually £1) for booking a room, while others ask you to pay a deposit of 10% which is deducted from your first night's bill. Details of TICs are given throughout the guide. There are also several websites that you can browse and book accommodation. Try www.visitscotland.com.

Accommodation will be your greatest expense, particularly if you are travelling on your own. Single rooms are in short supply and many places are reluctant to let a double room to one person, even when they're not busy. Single rooms are usually more than the cost per person for a double room and in some cases cost the same as two people sharing a double room. Finally, it is worth noting that many hotels and guesthouses in Orkney and Shetland close entirely in the winter.

Hotels, guesthouses and B&Bs Area tourist boards publish accommodation lists that include campsites, hostels, self-catering accommodation and VisitScotland-approved hotels, guesthouses and bed and breakfasts (B&Bs). Places participating in the VisitScotland system will have a plaque displayed outside which shows their grading, determined by a number of stars ranging from one to five. These reflect the level of facilities, as well as the quality of hospitality and service. However, do not assume that a B&B, guesthouse or hotel is no good because it is not listed by the tourist board. They simply don't want to pay to be included in the system, and some of them may offer better value.

Hotels At the lower end of the scale, there is often little to choose between cheaper hotels and guesthouses or B&Bs. The latter often offer higher standards of comfort and a more personal service, but many smaller hotels are really just guesthouses, and are often family-run and every bit as friendly. Note that some hotels, especially in town centres or in fishing ports, may also be rather noisy, as the bar can often be the social hub. Rooms in most mid-range to expensive hotels almost always have bathrooms en suite. Many upmarket hotels offer excellent room-only deals in the low season. An efficient last-minute hotel booking service is www.laterooms.com. Also note that many hotels offer cheaper rates for online booking through agencies such as www.lastminute.com.

Guesthouses Guesthouses are often large, converted family homes with up to five or six rooms. They tend to be slightly more expensive than B&Bs, charging between £30 and £50 per person per night, and though they are often less personal, usually provide better facilities, such as en suite bathroom, colour TV in each room and private parking. In many instances they are more like small budget hotels. Many guesthouses offer evening meals, though this may have to be requested in advance.

Bed and breakfasts (B&Bs) B&Bs provide the cheapest private accommodation. At the bottom end of the scale you can get a bedroom in a private house, a shared bathroom and a huge cooked breakfast for around £25-30 per person per night. Small B&Bs may only have one or two rooms to let, so it's important to book in advance during the summer season and on the islands where accommodation options are more limited. More upmarket B&Bs have en suite bathrooms and TVs in each room and usually charge from £30-35 per person per night. In general, B&Bs are more hospitable, informal, friendlier and offer better value than hotels. Many B&B owners are also a great source of local knowledge and can even provide OS maps for local walks. Many B&Bs in Orkney and Shetland offer dinner, bed and breakfast, which is useful as eating options are limited, especially on a Sunday.

Some places, especially in ferry ports, charge room-only rates, which are slightly cheaper and allow you to get up in time to catch an early morning ferry. However, this means that you miss out on a huge cooked breakfast. If you're travelling on a tight budget, you can eat as much as you can at breakfast time and save on lunch as you won't need to eat again until evening. Many B&B owners will even make up a packed lunch for you at a small extra cost.

Hostels
For those travelling on a tight budget, there are hostels offering cheap accommodation. These are also popular centres for backpackers and provide a great opportunity for

Price codes

Where to stay

££££	£160 and over	**£££**	£90-160
££	£50-90	**£**	under £50

Accommodation prices in this book are based on the cost for two people sharing a double room with en suite bathroom during the high season. Cheaper rooms with shared bathrooms are available in many hotels, guesthouses and B&Bs. Many places, particularly larger hotels, offer substantial discounts during the low season and at weekends. All places listed are recommended as providing good quality and value within their respective price category. Note that the vast majority of youth hostels and backpackers cost less than £20 per night.

Restaurants

£££	over £30 a head	**££**	£15-30	**£**	under £15 a head

The price ranges in this book are based on a two-course meal for one person (main course plus starter or dessert) without drinks. We have tried to include an equal number of choices in each category, though this is not always possible. All places listed are recommended as offering relatively good value, quality and standards of service within their respective price category.

meeting fellow travellers. Hostels have kitchen facilities for self-catering, and some include a continental breakfast in the price or provide cheap breakfasts and evening meals. Advance booking is recommended at all times and a credit card is often useful.

Scottish Youth Hostel Association (SYHA) The **Scottish Youth Hostel Association (SYHA)** ① *7 Glebe Cres, Stirling, T01786-891400, www.syha.org.uk*, is separate from the YHA in England and Wales. It has a network of over 60 hostels, which are often better and cheaper than those in other countries. They offer bunk-bed accommodation in single-sex dormitories or smaller rooms, kitchen and laundry facilities. The average cost is £12-20 per person per night. Some rural hostels are still strict on discipline and impose a 2300 curfew. Some larger hostels provide breakfasts for around £3 and three-course evening meals for £5-10. For all EU residents, adult membership costs £10 (students and under 16s are free), and can be obtained at the SYHA National Office, or at the first SYHA hostel you stay at. SYHA membership gives automatic membership of Hostelling International (HI). The SYHA produces a handbook (free with membership) giving details of all their youth hostels, including transport links. This can be useful as some hostels are difficult to get to without your own transport. You should always phone ahead, as many hostels are closed during the day and phone numbers are listed in this guide. Many hostels are closed during the winter, details are given in the SYHA Handbook. Youth hostel members are entitled to various discounts, including 20% off Edinburgh bus tours, 20% off Scottish Citylink tickets and 33% off the Orkney Bus (Inverness–Kirkwall).

Independent hostels Details of most independent hostels (or 'bunkhouses') can be found in the annual **Independent Hostel Guide**, www.independenthostelguide. com. The **Independent Backpackers Hostels of Scotland** is an association of nearly 100 independent hostels/bunkhouses throughout Scotland. This association has a programme

Wild camping

The Land Reform (Scotland) Act 2003, which together with the Scottish Access Code came into effect in February 2005, ensures Scotland offers walkers, canoeists, cyclists and campers some of the most liberal land access laws in Europe. Technically it means you have the 'right to roam' almost anywhere, although the emphasis is on 'responsible access' (see www.outdooraccess-scotland.com).

of inspection and lists members in their free 'Blue Guide'. Independent hostels tend to be more laid-back, with fewer rules and no curfew, and no membership is required. They all have dormitories, hot showers and self-catering kitchens. Some include continental breakfast, or provide cheap breakfasts. All these hostels are listed on their excellent website, www.hostel-scotland.co.uk. Shetland also has a network of unique camping böds, which provide very basic accommodation throughout the islands. For more information, see page 79, A böd for the night.

Campsites and self-catering
Campsites There are a number of small summer-only campsites around Orkney and Shetland, some of which are detailed in the text. If you plan to do a lot of camping, you should check out www.scottishcamping.com, www.visitscotland.com and www.visit.shetland.org.

Self-catering One of the most cost-effective ways to holiday in Orkney and Shetland is to hire a cottage with a group of friends.

The minimum stay is usually one week in the summer. Expect to pay at least £250-500 per week for a two-bedroom cottage. A good source of self-catering accommodation is the VisitScotland's guide, which lists over 1200 properties and is available to buy from any tourist office, but there are also dozens of excellent websites to browse. Amongst the best websites are the following: www.cottages-and-castles.co.uk, www.scottish-country-cottages.co.uk, www.cottages4you.co.uk, www.ruralretreats.co.uk, www.unique-cottages.co.uk and www.assc.co.uk.

The **National Trust for Scotland** ⓘ *28 Charlotte Sq, Edinburgh, T0844-493 2100, www.nts.org.uk*, owns many historic properties which are available for self-catering holidays, sleeping between two and 15 people. Prices start at around £400-500 per week in high season rising to £1000-1500 for the top of the range lodges.

Food and drink in Orkney and Shetland

Scottish cuisine has undergone a dramatic transformation in the last few decades and Scotland now boasts some of the most talented chefs, creating some of the best food in Britain. The heart of Scottish cooking is local produce, which includes the finest fish, shellfish, game, lamb, beef and vegetables, and a vast selection of traditionally made cheeses. What makes Scottish cooking so special is ready access to these foods. What could be better than enjoying an aperitif whilst watching your dinner being delivered by a local fisherman, knowing that an hour later you'll be enjoying the most delicious seafood?

Modern Scottish cuisine is now a feature of many of the top restaurants in the country. This generally means the use of local ingredients with foreign-influenced culinary styles, in particular French. International cuisine is also now a major feature on menus all over the country, influenced by the rise of Indian and Chinese restaurants in recent decades. In fact, so prevalent are exotic Asian and Oriental flavours that curry has now replaced fish and chips (fish supper) as the nation's favourite food.

Unfortunately, the wealth of eating options available on the mainland doesn't extend to Orkney and Shetland. Despite a ready supply of fresh local produce, especially seafood and Shetland lamb, the two archipelagos can feel like gastronomic backwaters. Another problem with eating out here is the very limited serving hours. It can be difficult finding food after 2000 and, in winter, many establishments will not open at all. With a few notable exceptions (which we've listed in this guide), the hotels and guesthouses are usually far and away the best and most reliable dining options. The one time when Shetland does celebrate its culinary potential is during an international food festival in June each year.

Food

Fish, meat and game form the base of many of the country's finest dishes. Scottish beef, particularly Aberdeen Angus, is the most famous in the world. This will, or should, usually be hung for at least four weeks and sliced thick. Game is also a regular feature of Scottish menus, though it can be expensive, especially venison (deer), but delicious and low in cholesterol. Pheasant and hare are also tasty, but grouse is, quite frankly, overrated.

Fish and seafood are fresh and plentiful, and you must not miss the chance to savour local mussels, prawns, oysters, scallops, langoustines, lobster or crab. Salmon is, of course, the most famous of Scottish fish, but you're more likely to be served the fish-farmed variety than 'wild' salmon, which has a more delicate flavour. Trout is also farmed extensively, but the standard of both remains high. Kippers are also a favourite delicacy. Proper fish and chips in Scotland are made with haddock; cod is for Sassenachs (the English) and cats.

Haggis has made something of a comeback, and small portions are often served as starters in fashionable restaurants. Haggis is traditionally eaten on Burns Night (25 January) in celebration of the great poet's birthday, when it is piped to the table and then slashed open with a sword at the end of a recital of Robert Burns' *Address to the Haggis*. Other national favourites feature names to relish: **cock-a-leekie** is a soup made from chicken, leeks and prunes; **cullen skink** is a delicious concoction of smoked haddock and potatoes; while at the other end of the scale of appeal is **hugga-muggie**, a Shetland dish using fish's stomach. There's also the delightfully named **crappit heids** (haddock heads stuffed with lobster) and **partan bree** (a soup made form giant crab's claws, cooked with rice). Rather more mundane is the ubiquitous **Scotch broth**, made with mutton stock, vegetables, barley, lentils and split peas, and **stovies**, which is a hearty mash of potato, onion and minced beef.

Waist-expanding puddings or desserts are a very important part of Scottish cooking and often smothered in butterscotch sauce or syrup. There is a huge variety, including **cranachan**, a mouth-watering mix of toasted oatmeal steeped in whisky, cream and fresh raspberries, and **Atholl Brose**, a similar confection of oatmeal, whisky and cream.

Eaten before pudding, in the French style, or afterwards, are Scotland's many home-produced cheeses, which have made a successful comeback in the face of mass-produced varieties. Many of the finest cheeses are produced on the islands, especially Arran, Mull, Islay and Orkney. **Caboc** is a creamy soft cheese rolled in oatmeal and is made in the Highlands.

Anyone staying at a hotel, guesthouse or B&B will experience the hearty **Scottish breakfast**, which includes bacon, egg, sausage, 'tattie scone' and black pudding (a type of sausage made with blood), all washed down with copious quantities of tea. Coffee is readily available everywhere, with most places now offering a selection of cappuccinos and café lattes. You may also be served kippers (smoked herring) or porridge, an erstwhile Scottish

Turn water into whisky

Malt whisky is made by first soaking dry barley in tanks of local water for two to three days. Then the barley is spread out on a concrete floor or placed in cylindrical drums and allowed to germinate for between eight and 12 days, after which it is dried in a kiln, heated by a peat fire. Next, the dried malt is ground and mixed with hot water in a huge circular vat called a 'mash tun'. A sugary liquid called 'wort' is then drawn from the porridge-like result and piped into huge containers where living yeast is stirred into the mix in order to convert the sugar in the wort into alcohol. After about 48 hours the 'wash' is transferred to copper pot stills and heated till the alcohol vaporizes and is then condensed by a cooling plant into distilled alcohol which is passed through a second still. Once distilled, the liquid is poured into oak casks and left to age for a minimum of three years, though a good malt will stay casked for at least eight years.

staple. Made with oatmeal and with the consistency of Italian polenta, it is traditionally eaten with salt, though heretics are offered sugar instead. Oatcakes (oatmeal biscuits) may also be on offer, as well as potato scones, baps (bread rolls) or bannocks (a sort of large oatcake). After such a huge cooked breakfast you probably won't feel like eating again until dinner.

Drink

Beer Beer is the alcoholic drink of choice in Scotland. The most popular type of beer is lager, which is generally brewed in the UK, even when it bears the name of an overseas brand, and is almost always weaker in both strength and character than the lagers in mainland Europe. However, examples of the older and usually darker type of beers, known as ales, are still widely available, and connoisseurs should try some of these as they are far more rewarding. Indeed, the best of them rival Scotland's whiskies as gourmet treats.

Traditionally, Scottish ales were graded by the shilling, an old unit of currency written as /-, according to strength. This system is still widely used by the older established breweries, though many of the newer independents and 'micros' have departed from it. 70/- beers at around 3.5% ABV (alcohol by volume), known as 'heavy', and 80/- beers (4.5% sometimes known as 'export'), are the most popular, while 60/-, 'light' (3-3.5%) is harder to find. Very strong 90/- beers (6.5% + ABV), known as 'wee heavies', are also brewed, mainly for bottling.

The market is dominated by the giant international brewers: Scottish Courage with its McEwans and Youngers brands; Interbrew with Calders and Carslberg; and Tetley with Tennents lagers. Tennents was the first British brewery to produce a continental-style lager commercially back in the 19th century, and, despite a competitive marketplace, remains a favourite for many Scots.

Much better are the ales from smaller independent breweries. Edinburgh's Caledonian is a world-class brewer producing many excellent beers, including a popular 80/- and a renowned golden hoppy ale, Deuchars IPA. Belhaven, an old, established family brewery in Dunbar, has some superb traditional beers including a malty 80/-, once marketed as the Burgundy of Scotland. Broughton, a microbrewery in the Borders, produces the fruity Greenmantle and an oatmeal stout. Another micro, Harvieston of Clackmannanshire (once an important brewing country) offers a wide and adventurous range of specialities, including Ptarmigan 80/- and a naturally brewed cask lager, Schiehallion. The Heather Ale Company, near Glasgow, has the spicy and unusual Fraoch (pronounced 'Frooch'), which is flavoured with real heather as well as hops.

Which whisky?

Opinions vary as to what are the best single malts and as to when you should drink them. As a rough guide, we would recommend a Speyside malt such as Glenmorangie or Glenlivet before dinner and one of the Islay malts – Ardbeg, Bowmore, Bunnahabhain (pronounced 'bun-a-haven'), Lagavulin, or the very wonderful Laphroaig (pronounced 'la-froig') – after dinner.

If the Islays are not to your taste, then you could try instead the versatile Highland Park from Orkney or perhaps Tamdhu or Aberlour from Speyside. Those eternal favourites, Glenfiddich and The Macallan, can be enjoyed at any time.

Draught beer in pubs and bars is served in pints, or half pints, and you'll pay between £3 and £3.70 for a pint (unless you discover a 'Happy Hour' offering good deals on drinks, usually for much more than one hour! Happy hours usually apply in late afternoon or early evening). In many pubs the basic ales are chilled under gas pressure like lagers, but the best ales, such as those from the independents, are 'real ales', still fermenting in the cask and served cool but not chilled (around 12°C) under natural pressure from a handpump, electric pump or air pressure fount. All Scottish beers are traditionally served with a full, creamy head.

Whisky There is no greater pleasure on an inclement evening than enjoying a malt whisky in front of a roaring log fire whilst watching the rain outside pelt down relentlessly. The roots of Scotland's national drink go back to the late 15th century, but it wasn't until the invention of a patent still in the early 19th century that distilling began to develop from small family-run operations to the large manufacturing business it has become today. Now more than 700 million bottles a year are exported, mainly to the United States, France, Japan and Spain.

There are two types of whisky: single malt, made only from malted barley; and grain, which is made from malted barley together with unmalted barley, maize or other cereals, and is faster and cheaper to produce. Most of the popular brands are blends of both types of whisky – usually 60-70% grain to 30-40% malt. These blended whiskies account for over 90% of all sales worldwide, and most of the production of single malts is used to add flavour to a blended whisky. Amongst the best-known brands of blended whisky are Johnnie Walker, Bells, Teachers and Famous Grouse. There's not much between them in terms of flavour and they are usually drunk with a mixer, such as water or soda.

Single malts are a different matter altogether. Each is distinctive and should be drunk neat to appreciate fully its subtle flavours, though some believe that the addition of water helps free the flavours. Single malts vary enormously. Their distinctive flavours and aromas are derived from the peat used for drying, the water used for mashing, the type of oak cask used and the location of the distillery. Single malts fall into four groups: Highland, Lowland, Campbeltown and Islay. There are over 40 distilleries to choose from, most offering guided tours. The majority are located around Speyside, in the northeast. The region's many distilleries include that perennial favourite, Glenfiddich, which is sold in 185 countries. Recommended alternatives are the produce of the beautiful and peaceful Isle of Islay, whose malts are lovingly described in terms of their peaty quality and the produce of the island known as 'Scotland in Miniature', Arran, whose 10-year-old malt, distilled in Lochranza, has won recent international acclaim. Scots tend to favour the 10-year-old Glenmorangie, while the most popular in the USA is The Macallan.

Entertainment in Orkney and Shetland

Bars and clubs

As in the rest of Britain, pubs are the main focus of social life and entertainment for most Scots. In many parts of Orkney and Shetland the local hotel bar is often the only watering hole for miles around. Visitors should also note that smoking is banned in pubs and bars, which means that those wishing to light up will have to step outside. Pubs are generally open Monday to Saturday from 1100 till 2300, and Sunday from 1100-1200 till 2230, though some close for a couple of hours between 1400 and 1600, which can be annoying on a wet afternoon.

Music

Folk music has a strong following in Orkney and Shetland and can often be heard in the pubs and bars. Both host annual folk festivals that attract international performers.

Festivals in Orkney and Shetland

There is a huge range of organized events held throughout Scotland every year, ranging in size and spectacle from the Edinburgh Festival, the largest arts festival in the world, to more obscure traditional events featuring ancient customs dating back many centuries. For all events in Scotland, by far and away the best website to visit is www.event scotland.org. The most popular tourist events are the **Highland Games** (or **Gatherings**), a series of competitions involving lots of kilts, bagpipes and caber-tossing, which are held across the Highlands and Islands, the northeast and Argyll from June to September.

Folk festivals take place all over the country, from Arran to Shetland, and are great fun. Musicians from all over Scotland gather to play the tunes, sing the songs and maybe, just maybe, drink the odd beer or two. Among the best of the folk festivals is the **Shetland Folk Festival**, usually held over a long weekend in April or early May. Details of local festivals are given in the listings sections of individual town and cities; also visit www.whatsonwhen.com.

Festivals

Jan New Year's Day A variety of ancient local celebrations take place, including the Kirkwall Ba' Game, a mixture of football and mud wrestling.

Up Helly-Aa Re-enactment of the ancient Viking fire festival held on Shetland on the last Tue in Jan, see pages 67 and 81.

Burns Night Burns suppers held on 25 Jan all over the country to celebrate the poet's birthday. Lots of haggis, whisky and poetry.

Jun St Magnus Festival, www. stmagnusfestival.com. High-brow cultural festival on Orkney.

Dec The Ba'(ball), in Kirkwall, www.bagame.com. See page 59.

31 Dec Hogmanay Old year's night, and the most important national celebration. Possible derivations of the word include Holag Monath, Anglo Saxon for 'holy month', and Hoog min dag, which is Dutch for 'great love day'.

Bank holidays

1 Jan New Year's Day

2 Jan Also a holiday in Scotland.

Mar-Apr Good Friday and Easter Monday

1 May May Day

May Victoria Day (the last Mon in May).

25 Dec Christmas Day

26 Dec Boxing Day

There are also local public holidays in spring and autumn. Dates vary from place to place. Banks are closed during these holidays, and sights and shops may be affected. Contact the relevant Area Tourist Board for more details.

Shopping in Orkney and Shetland

Scottish textiles, especially the **tartan** variety, are popular and worth buying. You can get hold of everything from a travelling rug to your own kilt outfit. Shops up and down the country can tell which clan your family belongs to and make you a kilt in that particular tartan. For the full outfit, including kilt, sporran, jacket, shoes and *skeann dhu* dagger, expect to pay in the region of £600, or more if you want elaborate accessories. **Harris Tweed** is also a good buy.

Knitwear is also good value and sold throughout Scotland. Shetland is a good place to find high-quality wool products. **Jewellery** is another popular souvenir and there are many excellent craft shops throughout the Highlands and Islands making beautiful jewellery with Celtic designs. **Glassware** is also popular, as well as pottery. You can order Scottish crafts at www.papastour.com.

Food is another good souvenir and not just the ubiquitous shortbread sold in tartan tins. If you haven't far to travel home, smoked salmon, or any other smoked product, is good value. And, of course, there's **whisky**. Most distilleries will refund the cost of their guided tour in the form of a discount voucher on a bottle of their brand whisky.

Shop hours are generally Monday to Saturday 0900-1730. Few shops are open on Sunday, most notably in the Outer Hebrides. Also note that in many rural areas there is an early-closing day when shops close at 1300. This varies from region to region, but the most common day is Wednesday.

Essentials A-Z

Accident and emergency

For police, fire brigade, ambulance and, in certain areas, mountain rescue or coastguard, T999 or T112.

Customs and duty free

Visitors from EU countries do not have to make a declaration to customs on entry into the UK. The limits for duty-paid goods from within the EU are 3200 cigarettes and 200 cigars, 10 litres of spirits, 20 litres of fortified wine, 90 litres of wine and 110 litres of beer. There is no longer any duty-free shopping. Visitors from non-EU countries are allowed to import 200 cigarettes, or 250 g of tobacco, 2 litres of wine, and 2 litres of fortified wine or 1 litre of spirits. There are various import restrictions, most of which should not affect the average tourist. There are tight quarantine restrictions which apply to animals brought from overseas (except for Ireland). For more information on British import regulations, contact **HM Customs and Excise**, Dorset House, Stamford St, London SE1 9PJ, T0845-010 9000, www.hmce.gov.uk.

Many goods in Britain are subject to a Value Added Tax (VAT) of 17.5%, with the major exception of books and food. Visitors from non-EU countries can save money through the Retail Export Scheme, which allows a refund of VAT on goods to be taken out of the country. Note that not all shops are participants in the scheme and that VAT cannot be reclaimed on hotel bills or other services.

Disabled travellers

For travellers with disabilities, visiting Orkney and Shetland independently can be a difficult business. While modern tourist attractions are accessible to wheelchairs, tours of historic buildings and archaeological sites may be tricky and finding accommodation remains problematic. Many large, new hotels do have disabled suites, but far too many B&Bs, guesthouses and smaller hotels remain ill-equipped to accept bookings from people with disabilities. However, through the work of organizations like **Disability Scotland** the Government is being pressed to further improve the Disability Discrimination Act and access to public amenities and transport. As a result, many buses and FirstScotRail's train services now accommodate wheelchair-users.

Wheelchair users, and blind or partially sighted people are automatically given 30-50% discount on train fares, and those with other disabilities are eligible for the Disabled Person's Railcard, which costs £20 per year and gives a third off most tickets. If you will need assistance at a railway station, call FirstScotRail before travelling on T0800-912 2901. There are no discounts on buses.

If you are disabled you should contact the travel officer of your national support organization. They can provide literature or put you in touch with travel agents specializing in tours for the disabled. **VisitScotland** produces a guide, 'Accessible Scotland', for disabled travellers, and many local tourist offices can provide accessibility details for their area. Alternatively call its national booking hotline on T0845-225 5121. A useful website is www.atlholidays. com, which specializes in organizing holidays for disabled travellers, recommends hotels with good facilities and can also arrange rental cars and taxis.

Useful organizations include:

Capability Scotland, ASCS, 11 Ellersly Rd, Edinburgh EH12 6HY, T0131-313 5510, or Textphone 0131-346 2529, www.capability-scotland.org.uk,

Holiday Care Service, T0845-124 9974, www. holidaycare.org.uk, www.tourismforall.org. uk. Both websites are excellent sources of information about travel and for identifying accessible accommodation in the UK.

Royal Association for Disability and Rehabilitation (RADAR), Unit 12, City Forum, 250 City Rd, London EC1V 8AF, T020-7250 3222, www.radar.org.uk. A good source of advice and information. It produces an annual *National Key Scheme Guide* for gaining access to over 6000 toilet facilities across the UK (£10.70 including P&P).

Electricity
The current in Britain is 240V AC. Plugs have 3 square pins and adapters are widely available.

Embassies and consulates
For a list of foreign embassies in London, consult www.gov.uk. Some nations, including the United States, Canada and several EU countries also have consulates in Scottish cities; these are listed at www.visitscotland.com/travel/information/embassies-consulates.

Health
No vaccinations are required for entry into Britain. Citizens of EU countries are entitled to free medical treatment at National Health Service (NHS) hospitals on production of a European Health Insurance Card (EHIC). For details, see the Department of Health website, www.dh.gov.uk/travellers. Also, Australia, New Zealand and several other non-EU European countries have reciprocal healthcare arrangements with Britain. Citizens of other countries will have to pay for all medical services, except accident and emergency care given at Accident and Emergency (A&E) Units at most (but not all) National Health Service hospitals. Health insurance is therefore strongly advised for citizens of non-EU countries.

Pharmacists can dispense only a limited range of drugs without a doctor's prescription. Most are open during normal shop hours. Local newspapers will carry lists of which are open late. Doctors' surgeries are usually open from around 0830-0900 till 1730-1800, though times vary. Outside surgery hours you can go to the casualty department of the local hospital for any complaint requiring urgent attention. For the address of the nearest hospital or doctors' surgery, www.nhs24.com.

You should encounter no major problems or irritations during your visit to Scotland. The only exceptions are the risk of hyperthermia if you're walking in difficult conditions.

Insurance
It's a good idea to take out some form of travel insurance, wherever you're travelling from. This should cover you for theft or loss of possessions and money, the cost of all medical and dental treatment, cancellation of flights, delays in travel arrangements, accidents, missed departures, lost baggage, lost passport, and personal liability and legal expenses. There are a variety of policies to choose from, so it's best to shop around to get the best price. Your travel agent can also advise you on the best deals available. **STA Travel**, www.statravel.co.uk, with branches nationwide, and other reputable student travel organizations often offer good-value travel policies. Another company worth calling for a quote is **Columbus Direct**, T0870-033 9988, www.columbusdirect.com. Older travellers should note that some companies won't cover people over 65 years old, or may charge high premiums. The best policies for older travellers are offered by **Age Concern**, T0800-009966, www.age concern.org.uk. Some other recommended travel insurance companies in North America include **Travel Guard**, T1-800 826 4919, www.travelguard.com; **Access America**, T1-800-284 8300, www.accessamerica.com; **Travel Insurance Services**, T1-800-937 1387, www.travelinsure.com; and **Travel Assistance International**, T1-800-821 2828, www.travelassistance.com.

Points to note: you should always read the small print carefully. Some policies exclude 'dangerous activities' such as scuba-diving, skiing, horse riding or even trekking. Not all policies cover ambulance, helicopter rescue or emergency flights home. Find out if your policy pays medical expenses direct to the hospital or doctor, or if you have to pay and then claim the money back later. If the latter applies, make sure you keep all records. Whatever your policy, if you are unfortunate enough to have something stolen, make sure you get a copy of the police report, as you will need this to substantiate your claim.

Internet
Even in the Highlands of Scotland, internet access is extensive. Every major town now has at least 1 internet café, with more springing up daily. Email works out much, much cheaper than phoning home and is also useful for booking hotels and tours, and for checking out information on the web. Many hotels now have Wi-Fi access and many hostels also offer internet access to their guests. Websites and email addresses are listed where appropriate in this guide. VisitScotland and area tourist boards have their own websites and these are given on page 28. In the absence of an internet cafe, try the public library or ask at the TIC.

Language
Though the vast majority of Scots speak English, to the untutored ear the Scottish dialect can be hard to understand, as many words and expressions are derived not from English but from Lowland Scots, or lallans, which is now recognized as a separate language as opposed to simply a regional dialect. In the Highlands and Islands, however, the accent is very clear and easy to understand.

Scotland's oldest surviving language is Scottish Gaelic (*Gaidhlig*, pronounced 'Gallic'), spoken by only about 2% of the population. Notably, a 2001 Census found Glasgow has the highest concentration of Gaelic speakers. Generally however, the Highlands, Outer Hebrides and Argyll have the greatest numbers of Gaelic-speaking inhabitants. Gaelic was never spoken in Orkney or Shetland. For many centuries the language of these islands was a variant of Old Norse known as Norrœna, or Norn. It was gradually superseded by Scots from the 15th century. Although the language no longer exists, remnants of it survive in local dialect words and Old Norse place names (see box, page 33).

Laundry
Kirkwall, Stromness and Lerwick have coin-operated launderettes. The average cost for a wash and tumble dry is about £3-4. A service wash, where someone will do your washing for you, costs around £5-6. In more remote areas, you'll have to rely on hostel and campsite facilities. An increasing number of SYHA hostels have excellent 'drying rooms' and washing facilities.

Money → *For up-to-date rates, visit xe.com.*
The British currency is the pound sterling (£), divided into 100 pence (p). Coins come in denominations of 1p, 2p, 5p, 10p, 20p, 50p, £1 and £2. Bank of England banknotes are legal tender in Scotland, in addition to those issued by the Bank of Scotland, Royal Bank of Scotland and Clydesdale Bank. These Scottish banknotes (bills) come in denominations of £5, £10, £20, £50 and £100; regardless of what you are told by shopkeepers in England, the notes are legal tender in the rest of Britain.

Banks
Kirkwall, Stromness and Lerwick have a branch of at least one of the big 4 high street banks – **Bank of Scotland**, **Royal Bank of Scotland**, **Clydesdale** and **TSB Scotland**. Bank opening hours are Mon-Fri from 0930 to between 1600 and 1700. Some larger branches may also be open later on Thu and on Sat mornings. In small and remote places, and on some islands, there may be a mobile bank which runs to a set timetable. This timetable will be available from the local post office.

Banks are usually the best places to change money and cheques. You can withdraw cash from selected banks and ATMs (or cashpoints as they are called in Britain) with your cash and credit card. Though using a debit or credit card is by far the easiest way of keeping in funds, you must check with your bank what the total charges will be; this can be as high as 4-5% in some cases. ATMs are few and far between and it is important to keep a ready supply of cash on you at all times; many guesthouses in the remoter reaches will still request payment in cash. Outside the ferry ports on most of the smaller islands, you won't find an ATM. Your bank will give you a list of locations where you can use your card. **Bank of Scotland** and **Royal Bank** take **Lloyds** and **Barclays** cash cards; **Clydesdale** takes **HSBC** and **National Westminster** cards. **Bank of Scotland**, **Clydesdale** and most building society cashpoints are part of the Link network and accept all affiliated cards. See also Credit cards below. In addition to ATMs, bureaux de change can be used outside banking hours. These can be found at the main airports. Note that some charge high commissions for changing cheques. Those at international airports, however, often charge less than banks and will change pound sterling cheques for free. Avoid changing money or cheques in hotels, as the rates are usually very poor.

Currency cards

If you don't want to carry lots of cash, prepaid currency cards allow you to preload money from your bank account, fixed at the day's exchange rate. They look like a credit or debit card and are issued by specialist money changing companies, such as Travelex and Caxton FX as well as the Post Office. You can top up and check your balance by phone, online and sometimes by text.

Credit cards

Larger hotels, shops and restaurants accept the major credit cards such as MasterCard and Visa and, less frequently, Amex, though some places may charge for using them. They will be less useful in more remote rural areas and smaller establishments such as B&Bs, which will often only accept cash or cheques.

Visa card holders can use the **Bank of Scotland**, **Clydesdale Bank**, **Royal Bank of Scotland** and TSB ATMs; Access/MasterCard holders, the Royal Bank and Clydesdale; Amex card holders, the Bank of Scotland.

Traveller's cheques

The safest way to carry money is in traveller's cheques. These are available for a small commission from all major banks. **American Express (Amex)**, **Visa** and **Thomas Cook** cheques are widely accepted and are the most commonly issued by banks. You'll normally have to pay commission again when you cash each cheque. This will usually be 1%, or a flat rate. No commission is payable on Amex cheques cashed at Amex offices, www.americanexpress.co/feefree. Make sure you keep a record of the cheque numbers and the cheques you've cashed separate from the cheques themselves, so that you can get a full refund of all uncashed cheques should you lose them. It's best to bring sterling cheques to avoid changing currencies twice. Also note that in Britain traveller's cheques are rarely accepted outside banks or foreign exchange bureaux, so you'll need to cash them in advance and keep a good supply of ready cash.

Money transfers

If you need money urgently, the quickest way to have it sent to you is to have it wired to the nearest bank via **Western Union**, T0800-833 833, www.westernunion. co.uk, or **Money-gram**, T0800-8971 8971. Charges are on a sliding scale; ie it will cost proportionately less to wire out more money. Money can also be wired by **Thomas Cook**, www.thomasexchangeglobal.co.uk, or transferred via a bank draft, but this can take up to a week.

Cost of travelling

The Highlands and Islands of Scotland can be an expensive place to visit, and prices are higher in more remote parts, but there is plenty of budget accommodation available and backpackers will be able to keep their costs down. Petrol is a major expense and won't just cost an arm and a leg but also the limbs of all remaining family members. Expect to pay up to 15p per litre more than in central and southern parts of Scotland and never pass a fuel station if running low as the next one might be hours away.

The minimum daily budget required, if you're staying in hostels or camping, cycling, and cooking your own meals, will be around £25-30 per person per day. If you start using public transport and eating out occasionally that will rise to around £35-40. Those staying in slightly more upmarket B&Bs or guesthouses, eating out every evening at pubs or modest restaurants and visiting tourist attractions, such as castles or museums, can expect to pay around £60-80 per day. If you also want to hire a car and use ferries to visit the islands, and eat well, then costs will rise considerably and you'll be looking at least £80-100 per person per day. Single travellers will have to pay more than ½ the cost of a double room in most places, and should budget on spending around 60-70% of what a couple would spend.

Museums, galleries and historic houses

Many of Orkney and Shetland's tourist attractions are open only from Easter-Oct. Full details of opening hours and admission charges are given in the relevant sections of this guide.

Over 100 of Scotland's most prestigious sights, and 75,000 ha of beautiful countryside, are cared for by the **National Trust for Scotland** (NTS), 26-31 Charlotte Sq, Edinburgh EH2 4ET, T0844-493 2100, www.nts.org.uk. National Trust properties are indicated in this guide as 'NTS', and entry charges and opening hours are given for each property.

Historic Scotland (HS), Longmore House, Salisbury Pl, Edinburgh EH9 1SH, T0131-668 8600, www.historic-scotland.gov.uk, manages more than 330 of Scotland's most important castles, monuments and other historic sites. Admission charges and opening hours are also given in this guide. Historic Scotland offers an **Explorer Pass** which allows free entry to 70 of its properties. A 3-day pass (can be used over 5 consecutive days) costs £29, concessions £24, family £58, 7-day pass (valid for 14 days) £38, £31, £76. It can save a lot of money, especially in Orkney, where most of the monuments are managed by Historic Scotland (see page 36).

Many other historic buildings are owned by local authorities, and admission is cheap, or in many cases free. Most fee-paying attractions give a discount or concession for senior citizens, the unemployed, full-time students and children under 16 (those under 5 are admitted free everywhere). Proof of age or status must be shown. Many of Scotland's stately homes are still owned and occupied by the landed gentry, and admission is usually between £5 and £10.

Post

Most post offices are open Mon-Fri 0900-1730 and Sat 0900-1230 or 1300. Smaller sub-post offices are closed for an hour at lunch (1300-1400) and many of them operate out of a shop. Post offices keep the same ½-day closing times as shops.

Stamps can be bought at post offices, but also from vending machines outside, and also at many newsagents. A 1st-class letter weighing up to 100 g to anywhere in the UK costs 60p and should arrive the following day, while 2nd-class letters weighing up to 100 g cost 50p and take 2-4 days. For more information about Royal Mail postal services, call T08457-740740, or visit www.royalmail.com.

Safety

Incidences of serious crime in Highlands and Islands tend to be the exception rather than the rule and are so rare that they always make front page news. In fact, if someone failed to say 'good morning' – heaven forfend – it would provoke such an outcry that locals would be talking about little else for weeks to come. Orkney has the lowest crime rate in the UK. In most island communities people don't even lock their doors at night, and will even leave their car keys still in the lock. The major safety issue relates to the unpredictable weather conditions. Everyone should be aware of the need for caution and proper preparation when walking or cycling.

Telephone → *Country code +44.*
Useful numbers: operator T100; international operator T155; directory enquiries T192; overseas directory enquiries T153.

Roaming charges for smartphones and tablets have come down drastically and the EU is planning to ban mobile roaming charges from July 2014. Sightings of public payphones are about as frequent as Nessie, so don't rely on being able to find a payphone wherever you go. BT payphones take either coins (20p, 50p and £1) or phonecards, which are available at newsagents and post offices displaying the BT logo. These cards come in denominations of £2, £3, £5 and £10. Some payphones also accept credit cards.

For most countries (including Europe, USA and Canada) calls are cheapest Mon-Fri between 1800 and 0800 and all day Sat-Sun. For Australia and New Zealand it's cheapest to call 1430-1930 and 2400-0700 every day. Area codes are not needed if calling from within the same area. Any number prefixed by 0800 or 0500 is free to the caller; 08457 numbers are charged at local rates and 08705 numbers at the national rate. To call Scotland from overseas, dial 011 from USA and Canada, 0011 from Australia and 00 from New Zealand, followed by 44, then the area code, minus the first zero, then the number. To call overseas from Scotland dial 00 followed by the country code. Country codes include: Australia 61; Ireland 353; New Zealand 64; South Africa 27; USA and Canada 1.

Time
Greenwich Mean Time (GMT) is used from late Oct to late Mar, after which time the clocks go forward an hour to British Summer Time (BST). GMT is 5 hrs ahead of US Eastern Standard Time and 10 hrs behind Australian Eastern Standard Time.

Tipping
Believe it or not, people in Scotland do leave tips. In a restaurant you should leave a tip of 10-15% if you are satisfied with the service. If the bill already includes a service charge, you needn't add a further tip. Tipping is not normal in pubs or bars. Taxi drivers will expect a tip for longer journeys, usually of around 10%; and most hairdressers will also expect a tip. As in most other countries, porters, bellboys and waiters in more up-market hotels rely on tips to supplement their meagre wages.

Tour operators
There are many companies offering general interest or special interest tours of Scotland. Travel agents will have details, or you can check the small advertisements in the travel sections of newspapers, or contact VisitBritain or VisitScotland for a list of operators.

In the UK
Cape Adventure, Ardmore, Rhiconich, by Lairg, Sutherland IV27 4RB, T01971-521006, www.capeventure.co.uk. Whether you want to spend a weekend sea kayaking and climbing, or a week trekking the wilds of northwest Scotland, this acclaimed operator offers bags of adventure for families and individuals.
c-n-do Scotland, 32 Stirling Enterprise Park, Stirling, T01786-445703, www.cndoscotland. com. A highly reputable walking holiday specialist with diverse itineraries across the Highlands and Islands.

Haggis Adventures, 11 Blackfriars St, Edinburgh EH1 1NB, T0131-557 9393, www.haggisadventures.com. Award-winning operator specializing in offering a variety of day and week-long tours for independent travellers including backpackers.

Macbackpackers, Edinburgh, T0131-558 9900, www.macbackpackers.com. Well-established tour operator for independent budget travellers with 2-5 day minibus tours ranging from £69-165 of the Highlands and Islands that depart from Edinburgh and use a network of hostel accommodation.

National Trust for Scotland (NTS), 28 Charlotte Sq, Edinburgh EH2 4ET, T0844-4932100, www.nts.org.uk. With over 300 historic properties and landscapes under its care, Scotland's largest conservation charity also offers the chance to stay in historic cottages and country houses or participate in archaeological digs and conservation weekends.

North-West Frontiers, Viewfield, Strathpeffer IV14 9DS, T01997-421474, www.nwfrontiers.com. Offers a good range of guided and self-guided hiking and walking tours across north of Scotland and islands including a trip focused on Assynt's world reknown geology. See also www.highland-tours.co.uk.

Rabbie's Trail Burners, 207 High St, Edinburgh, T0131-226 3133, www.rabbies.com. From Glasgow and Edinburgh runs insightful 1- and multi-day, minibus based tours of the Highlands and Islands for independent travellers.

Scottish Cycling Holidays, 87 Perth St, Blairgowrie, T01250-876100, www.scotcycle.co.uk. Perthshire based operator that for over 30 years has offered guided and self-guided 2-day to 8-day pedal powered trips throughout Scotland. Prices vary; eg, the 5 day/4 night Great Glen way costs £280 pp inc equipment hire and accommodation.

Timberbush Tours, 555 Castlehill, Edinburgh, T0131-226 6066, www.timberbush-tours. co.uk. Award winning, family-run run operator offering a variety of 1-3 day guided coach tours around the country.

Walkabout Scotland, 2F2, 70 Strathearn Rd, Edinburgh EH9 2AF, T0845-686 1344, www.walkaboutscotland.com. Day, weekend and week-long walking tours around Scotland.

Wilderness Scotland, T0131-625 6635, www.wildernessscotland.com. Specialist Edinburgh-based adventure tour operator offering excellent walking, climbing, kayaking, hiking and photographic trips into Scotland's wild places, plus tailor-made and self-guided trips.

In North America

Abercrombie & Kent, T1-800-554 7016, www.abercrombiekent.com. General sighseeing tours.

Golf International, T1-800-833 1389, www.golfinternational.com. American-based operator offering golfing tours of Scotland.

Celtic Golf, T1-609-465 0600, www.celticgolf.com. Organizes golfing packages from the USA.

Travel and Company, T1-800-888 2247, www.travelandcompany.com. Boston-based operator offering a 9-day Links and Leisure tour.

Tourist information
Tourist information centres

Tourist offices – called tourist information centres (TICs) – can be found in most Scottish towns. Their addresses, phone numbers and opening hours are listed in the relevant sections of this book. Opening hours vary depending on the time of year, and many of the smaller offices are closed during the winter months. All tourist offices provide information on accommodation, public transport, local attractions and restaurants, as well as selling books, local guides, maps and souvenirs. Many also have free street plans and leaflets describing local walks. They can also book accommodation for you, for a small fee.

Finding out more

The best way of finding out more information for your trip to Scotland is to contact VisitScotland (aka the Scottish Tourist Board), www.visitscotland.com. Alternatively, you can contact VisitBritain, the organization that is responsible for tourism throughout the British Isles. Both organizations can provide a wealth of free literature and information such as maps, city guides and accommodation brochures. If particularly interested in ensuring your visit coincides with a major festival or sporting event, it's also worthwhile having a look at EventScotland's website, www.eventscotland.org. Travellers with special needs should also contact VisitScotland or their nearest VisitBritain office. If you want more detailed information on a particular area, click through to the specific tourist boards via the VisitScotland website.

VisitScotland, Ocean Point One, 94 Ocean Drive, Edinburgh EH6 6JH, T0845-225 5121, www.visitscotland.com (the phone number is the national booking line for accommodation or to order a brochure). VisitScotland also operates offices around 6 key regional areas.

Also consult www.visitorkney.com and www.shetland.org.

Useful websites
Travel and leisure

www.aboutscotland.co.uk Online resource for information on accommodation.

www.bbc.co.uk/scotland Ideal for grasping key information about news, views, events taking place across Scotland and the weather.

www.britannia.com A huge UK travel site. Click on 'Scotland guide' for a massive selection of subjects plus links to various sites including newspapers.

www.scotland-info.co.uk Good for local information on hotels, shops and restaurants.

www.scotlandbybike If you've ever dreamed of touring the Highlands and Islands on a classy motorbike this operator ensures you can enjoy guided tours, ride pillion or simply take off by yourself.

www.uktrail.com Very useful for pinpointing budget style hostels around Scotland.

www.undiscoveredscotland.com Another good online source of information for details about villages and towns across the country including their history and with recommendations for accommodation.

Outdoors

www.golfscotland.co.uk Everything you need to know about golf in Scotland.

www.goodbeachguide.co.uk Reveals the 22 of 108 beaches in the North of Scotland that passed stringent 'MCS recommended' water quality standards.

www.magicseaweed.com The latest surf conditions around Scotland and the world.

www.mwis.org.uk The weather in Scotland's mountains can change in minutes so before you head into the hills log on for the latest forecast.

www.sustrans.org.uk Official site of the charity that co-ordinates the National Cycle Network. The clickable map lets you zoom in on sections of the route and reveals a network stretching from the Scottish Borders to the Shetland Islands. Happy pedalling!

www.walkingworld.com Perhaps the best directory of British walks though you have to pay to download their detailed maps.

www.walkscotland.com This is a fairly comprehensive site with suggested walks, contacts and practical information for hikers and climbers.

History, politics and culture

www.ceolas.org Celtic music site with lots of information and sounds.

www.electricscotland.com Massive directory with lots of information on clans, travel, etc. In-depth history pages.

www.scotchwhisky.net Everything you ever wanted to know about the 'water of life'.

www.scotland.gov.uk Updates on government affairs in Scotland.
www.scottish.parliament.uk Easy to use guide to the Scottish Parliament.
www.smws.co.uk Worldwide whisky association with its roots in Scotland, offering members the chance to sample rare whiskies.

Visas and immigration
Visa regulations are subject to change, so it is essential to check with your local British embassy, high commission or consulate before leaving home. Citizens of all European countries – except Albania, Bosnia Herzegovina, Kosovo, Macedonia, Moldova, Turkey, Serbia and all former Soviet republics (other than the Baltic states) – require only a passport to enter Britain and can generally stay for up to 3 months. Citizens of Australia, Canada, New Zealand, South Africa or the USA can stay for up to 6 months, providing they have a return ticket and sufficient funds to cover their stay. Citizens of most other countries require a visa from the commission or consular office in the country of application.

The **Foreign and Commonwealth Office (FCO)**, T0207-270 1500, **www.fco. gov.uk**, has an excellent website, which provides details of British immigration and visa requirements. Also the Home Office UK Border Agency is responsible for UK immigration matters and its website is a good place to start for anyone hoping

visit, work, study or emigrate to the UK: www.ukba.homeoffice.gov.uk.

For visa extensions also contact the **Home Office UK Border Agency** via the above number or its website. The agency can also be reached at Lunar House, Wellesley Rd, Croydon, London CR9. Citizens of Australia, Canada, New Zealand, South Africa or the USA wishing to stay longer than 6 months will need an Entry Clearance Certificate from the British High Commission in their country. For more details, contact your nearest British embassy, consulate or high commission, or the Foreign and Commonwealth Office in London.

Weights and measures
Imperial and metric systems are both in use. Distances on roads are measured in miles and yards, drinks poured in pints and gills, but generally, the metric system is used elsewhere.

Women travellers
Travelling in Orkney and Shetland is neither easier nor more difficult for women than travelling in other parts of the UK. Generally speaking, islanders are friendly and courteous and even lone women travellers should experience nothing unpleasant, however, common sense dictates that single women would do well to avoid hitching on their own in the middle of nowhere. In the main towns, the usual precautions need to be taken and you should avoid walking in quiet, unlit streets at night.

Contents

Footprint features

Orkney

Orkney may be separated from the north coast of Scotland by a mere six miles of the notoriously changeable waters of the Pentland Firth, but to the fiercely independent Orcadians 'Mainland' means the largest of the Orkney islands and not the Scottish mainland. Mainland is also the site of the two main towns and ferry terminals: the capital Kirkwall and the beautiful old fishing port of Stromness. Orkney has the densest concentration of prehistoric monuments in Britain and Mainland is where you'll find many of these archaeological relics: the Stones of Stenness, Maes Howe, the Broch of Gurness and the remarkable Neolithic village of Skara Brae, all of which give Orkney a rare continuity of past and present. Aside from Mainland, there are a dozen smaller islands to explore, including Hoy, with its wild, spectacular coastal scenery. The even more remote northerly islands offer miles of deserted beaches and nothing but the calls of birds to shatter the peace and quiet. Quiet also describes the taciturn locals. They aren't unfriendly – quite the opposite, in fact – but it's said that Orcadians will rarely use one word where none will do.

Arriving in Orkney

Getting there

There are direct flights to Kirkwall airport Monday to Saturday from Aberdeen, Edinburgh, Glasgow, Inverness, Shetland and Bergen in Norway, with connections to London Heathrow, Birmingham, Manchester and Belfast. These are operated by Flybe/Loganair and can be booked through **Flybe** ⓘ *T0871-700 2000, www.flybe.com*, or **Loganair** ⓘ *T01856-886210, www.loganair.co.uk*.

There are several ferry routes to Orkney: Aberdeen to Kirkwall (six to seven hours); Scrabster, near Thurso, to Stromness (90 minutes, the boat sails close to the Old Man of Hoy); John o'Groats to Burwick, on South Ronaldsay (from May to September, 40 minutes) and Gill's Bay, near John o'Groats, to St Margaret's Hope. There's also an 'Orkney Bus', which leaves daily from Inverness, direct to Kirkwall. ➨ *For further details, see Transport, page 60.*

Getting around

There are flights from Kirkwall to many of the islands which are operated by Loganair (see above). They are very reasonable, costing £36 return to North Ronaldsay and Papa Westray,

Learning the lingo

Despite the disappearance of the Norse language, many of the Viking place names have survived. Here are some of the most common Old Norse elements which will help explain the meaning of many place names:

a(y)	island	holm	small island
a, o	stream	howe	mound
aith	isthmus	kirk	church
ayre	beach	lax	salmon
bard	headland	ler	mud, clay
bister	farm	lyng	heather
brae, brei	broad	minn	mouth
fell, field	hill	mool, noup	headland
fors	waterfall	setter	farm
garth	farm	thing	parliament
geo	creek	toft	house site
grind	gate	voe	sea inlet
ham(n)	anchorage	wick, vik	bay

and £39 return to Eday, Sanday, Stronsay and Westray. There are also inter-island saver flights costing £21 return, and excursion flights (requiring a minimum of one night's stay at the destination), which cost £15 return. There are also sightseeing flights in July and August costing £39, which can only be booked 30 minutes prior to departure.

Orkney Ferries ① T01856-872044, www.orkneyferries.co.uk, operates daily car and passenger ferries to Rousay, Egilsay and Wyre from Tingwall with return fares costing £8.30, concessions and children £4.20 and £26.40 per car. Ferries to Shapinsay from Kirkwall also cost £8.30/4.20/26.40. Ferries to Eday, Stronsay, Sanday, Westray and Papa Westray from Kirkwall cost £16.20, concessions and children £8.10 and £38.30 per car. To Graemsay and Hoy from Stromness and to Hoy and Flotta from Houton costs £8.30, concessions £4.20 and £26.40 per car. An inter-island fare for the North Islands is £8.10, concessions and children £4 and £30.40 per car. If travelling by car, book ferry journeys in advance. All these prices are return with single fares 50% of the return price. A seven-day Island Explorer Ticket can be purchased for the North and South Isles, costing £42, concessions and children £21. Bikes travel free of charge.

Only the main population centres on Mainland are served by public transport, and having a car is highly recommended to visit many of the most interesting sights. Bringing a car to Orkney is expensive, but there are several car hire firms on the Mainland and on the other islands. An alternative could be taking a bike. Orkney is relatively flat and most of its roads are quiet, which makes it ideal for touring on two wheels, though the wind can make it difficult if it's blowing in the wrong direction. Bicycles can be hired in Kirkwall, Stromness and on many of the other islands. Those with limited time may prefer to book a tour of the islands. ►► *For further details, see What to do, page 59, and Transport, page 60.*

Tourist information

Orkney Tourist Board ① www.visitorkney.com, has tourist offices in Kirkwall and Stromness. They will book accommodation for you, or provide a list of what's available, though many

Orkney

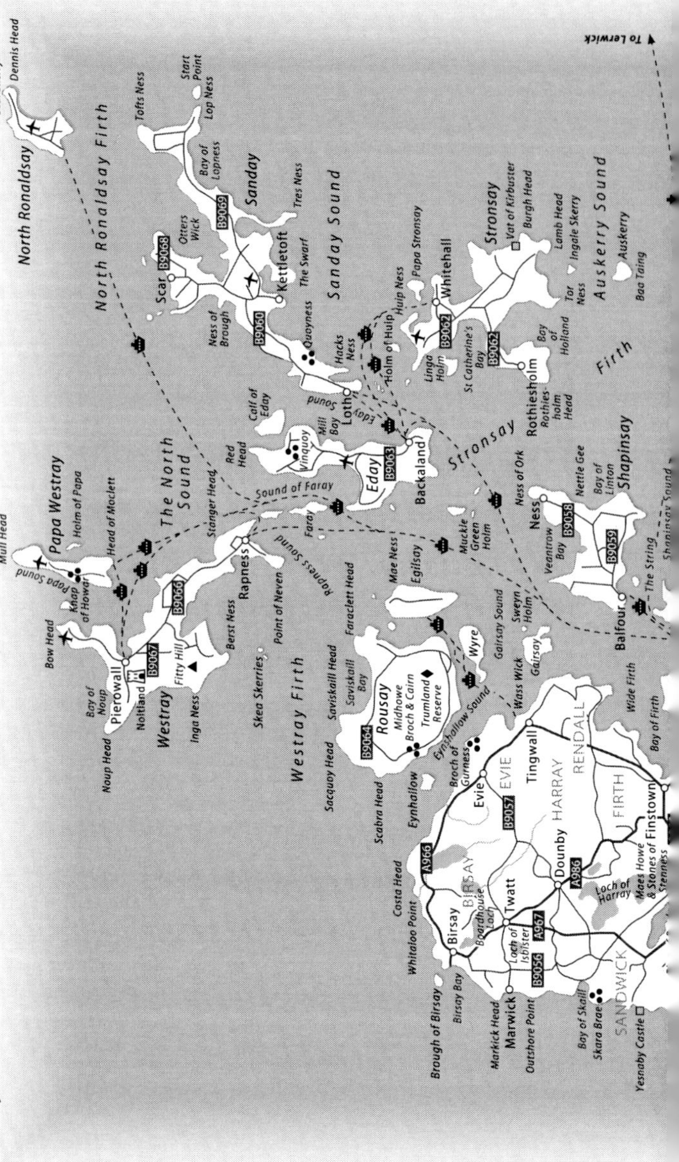
North Ronaldsay
Seal Skerry
Dennis Head
North Ronaldsay Firth
Tofts Ness
Start Point
Lop Ness
Bay of Lopness
Sanday
Tres Ness
Otters Wick
Scar
B9068
B9069
Kettletoft
The Swarf
Sanday Sound
Ness of Brough
B9060
Quoyness
Hacks Ness
Loth
Eday Sound
Calf of Eday
Red Head
Mill Bay
Vinquoy
Eday
B9063
Backaland
Papa Westray
Mull Head
Holm of Papa
Head of Moclett
Papa Sound
Knap of Howar
The North Sound
Stanger Head
Sound of Faray
Faray
Rapness
Rapness Sound
B9066
Bow Head
Pierowall
B9067
Noltland
Fitty Hill
Berst Ness
Point of Neven
Bay of Noup
Noup Head
Westray
Inga Ness
Skea Skerries
Westray Firth
Faraclett Head
Mae Ness
Egilsay
Muckle Green Holm
Saviskaill Head
Saviskaill Bay
Rousay
Midhowe Broch & Cairn
Trumland Reserve
B9064
Wyre
Gairsay Sound
Sweyn Holm
Gairsay
Wass Wick
Eynhallow Sound
Sacquoy Head
Scabra Head
Eynhallow
Broch of Gurness
Evie
EVIE
B9057
Tingwall
RENDALL
HARRAY
FIRTH
Costa Head
A966
Dounby
A986
Loch of Harray
Maes Howe & Stones of Stenness
Finstown
Whitaloo Point
Birsay
BIRSAY
Boardhouse Loch
Twatt
A967
Loch of Isbister
B9056
Brough of Birsay
Birsay Bay
Marwick Head
Marwick
Outshore Point
Bay of Skaill
Skara Brae
SANDWICK
Yesnaby Castle
Papa Stronsay
Huip Ness
Holm of Huip
Whitehall
B9062
Linga Holm
St Catherine's Bay
Stronsay
Vat of Kirbuster
Burgh Head
Lamb Head
Ingale Skerry
Tor Ness
Auskerry Sound
Auskerry
Baa Taing
Bay of Holland
Rothiesholm
Rothiesholm Head
Stronsay Firth
Ness of Ork
Nettle Gee
Bay of Linton
Shapinsay
Ness
B9058
Veantrow Bay
B9059
The String
Shapinsay Sound
Balfour
Wide Firth
Bay of Firth
To Lerwick

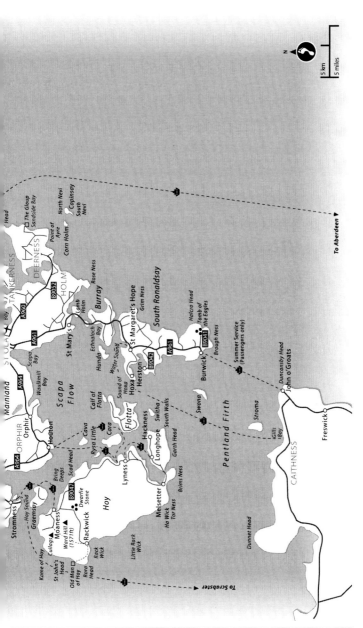

B&Bs are not included in the tourist board scheme. They can also provide information on various sights, walks and the islands' wildlife. Those wishing to leave Mainland and visit the smaller islands should pick up a free copy of the tourist board's excellent information and travel guide, *The Islands of Orkney*. Packed with information, their *Orkney, irresistible islands* brochure is also worth a browse.

Many of Orkney's monuments are managed by **Historic Scotland** ① *www.historic scotland.gov.uk*. They include the Bishop and Earl's Palaces, Broch of Gurness, Maes Howe, Skara Brae and Skaill House, Brough of Birsay and Hackness Martello Tower. If you plan to visit all or most of these sights, it is cheaper to buy a **Historic Scotland Orkney Explorer Pas**s which costs £18 for adults, £14.40 concessions, £10.80 child and £36 for a family.

Kirkwall → *For listings, see pages 53-62. Phone code 01856. Population 7000.*

Orkney's rugged, Nordic-feeling capital is built around a wide sheltered bay and is the main departure point for ferries to the northern islands. First impressions are a little misleading, as the harbour area has been blighted by modern development. More appealing, however, are the narrow winding streets and lanes of the old town, which has not changed much over the centuries. There are many houses dating from the 16th, 17th and 18th centuries, as well as Kirkwall's greatest attraction, its magnificent cathedral, the finest medieval building in northern Scotland.

Arriving in Kirkwall

Getting there and around The airport ① *T01856-886210 (information desk) or T0871-700 2000 (Flybe desk)*, is three miles southeast of Kirkwall on the A960. There are no buses to and from town. A taxi will cost around £6. **Northlink Ferries** ① *T08456-000449, www.northlinkferries.co.uk*, sail from Aberdeen to Kirkwall (six hours) on Tuesday, Thursday, Saturday and Sunday at 1700. Northlink Ferries also sail from Lerwick (Shetland) to Kirkwall on Monday, Wednesday and Friday at 1730, the journey takes seven hours and 45 minutes. Cars should be booked in advance and all passengers must check in at least 30 minutes before departure. **John o'Groats Ferries** ① *T01955-611353, www.jogferry.co.uk*, run a ferry from John o'Groats to Burwick, with a bus connection to Kirkwall (45 minutes). The ferries leave twice a day and four times a day between June and August. The journey takes 40 minutes. John o'Groats Ferries also operate the Orkney Bus, a daily direct bus/ferry/bus service between Inverness and Kirkwall, via John o'Groats. It leaves Inverness at 0715 and 1420 from 1 June to 31 August and costs £55 return, advance booking is essential. The bus station is five minutes' walk west of the town centre.

The town is compact and it's easy to get around on foot. The main street changes its name from Bridge Street to Albert Street, then to Broad Street and Victoria Street as it twists its way south from the busy harbour. The cathedral is on Broad Street, and most of the shops and banks are on Broad Street and Albert Street. ➡ *For further details, see Transport, page 60.*

Tourist information On Broad Street, near the cathedral, is the very helpful TIC ① *T01856-872856, www.visitorkney.com, Jun-Aug daily 0830-2000, Sep-Mar Mon-Fri 0900-1700 Sat 1000-1600, closed Sun.* Services they provide include booking accommodation and changing money; they also have various useful free leaflets including *The Islands of Orkney*, the *Kirkwall Heritage Guide* and *The Peedie Guide* – a pocket-sized guide to eating, drinking, shopping and entertainment. They also stock a wide range of guidebooks and maps, and have details of forthcoming events. Another good source is the weekly newspaper *The Orcadian*.

Places in Kirkwall

The town's outstanding sight is the huge and impressive red sandstone **St Magnus Cathedral** ① *T01856-874894, Apr-Sep Mon-Sat 0900-1800, Sun 1300-1800, Oct-Mar Mon-Sat 0900-1300, 1400-1700, free,* built by masons who had worked on Durham Cathedral in the north of England. It was founded in 1137 by Rognvald Kolson, Earl of Orkney, in memory of his uncle, Magnus Erlendson, who was slain by his cousin, Haakon Paulson,

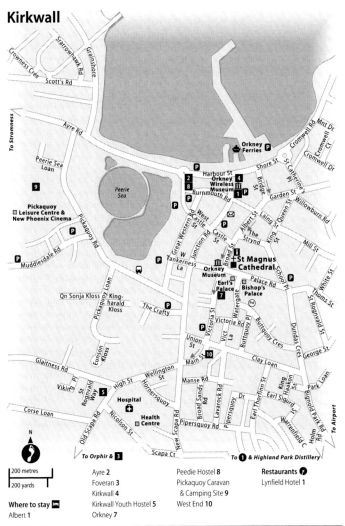

Kirkwall

200 metres	Ayre **2**	Peedie Hostel **8**	Restaurants ❼
200 yards	Foveran **3**	Pickaquoy Caravan	Lynfield Hotel **1**
	Kirkwall **4**	& Camping Site **9**	
Where to stay 🛏	Kirkwall Youth Hostel **5**	West End **10**	
Albert **1**	Orkney **7**		

Scandanavian settlements

The history of Orkney and Shetland is bound up with the history of the Vikings, who first came to the islands in the latter half of the ninth century and stayed for about 650 years. This was part of a great Viking expansion westwards, and in less than a century emigrants from Norway and Denmark settled in Orkney, Shetland, Iceland, Greenland, Caithness, the Western Isles, Isle of Man and parts of Ireland and the northern half of England.

In 872 the King of Norway set up a Norse earldom in Orkney, from which the Vikings ruled Orkney, Shetland and the Western Isles and took part in raids around Britain and Europe, creating the popular image of Vikings as aggressive, bloodthirsty invaders. At home, however, they lived a peaceful life, adhering to the laws of their parliament, the 'thing', and many converted to Christianity.

In the late 14th century Norway, Denmark and Sweden were united under a Danish king. In 1469 the Royal estates and prerogatives in Orkney and Shetland were pledged to Scotland as part of the marriage dowry of Margaret, daughter of the King of Denmark, on her marriage to Prince James of Scotland, later to become King James III. Orkney and Shetland were to revert to rule by the kings of Norway when the debt was paid, but the pledge was never redeemed and the islands remained under Scottish control.

Soon after assuming control, the Scots began to change the old Norse laws, which they had agreed to maintain, and Scottish influence grew. In 1564 Mary, Queen of Scots granted the control and revenues from Orkney and Shetland to her half-brother, Robert Stewart. His prime motivation, however, was to extract as much money as possible through taxes. He was succeeded by his son, the infamous Patrick Stewart, who demanded even more rents, dues and fines. Earl Patrick eventually got his come-uppance when he was executed in Edinburgh for treason, but the changes he had made continued and Scots and English gradually began to usurp Old Norse as the native language of the islands.

on Egilsay in 1115. Magnus was buried at Birsay and it is said that heavenly light was seen over his grave. It soon became a shrine, attracting pilgrims from as far afield as Norway. Magnus was canonized in 1133, and four years later his nephew commissioned construction of the cathedral. The building wasn't completed until the 14th century. Major additions have been made over the centuries, the most recent of which was a new west window for the nave, to celebrate the cathedral's 850th anniversary in 1987. The bones of St Magnus now lie in the north choir pillar, while those of St Rognvald lie in the south one. There's also a memorial to John Rae, the 19th-century Arctic explorer who is buried in the graveyard, as well as a monument to the 833 men of the *HMS Royal Oak* who died when it was torpedoed in Scapa Flow in 1939.

Looming impressively nearby are the ruins of the **Bishop's Palace** ① *T01856-875461, entry by combined ticket with Earl's Palace*, built in the 12th century as the first Kirkwall residence of the Bishop of Orkney. Here King Haakon of Norway died in 1263 after his defeat at the Battle of Largs. The palace was repaired and extended in the mid-16th century by Bishop Reid, and most of what you see dates from that period. There's a good view of the town from the top of the 'Moosie Too'r'.

The adjacent **Earl's Palace** ① *T01856-875461, Apr-Sep daily 0930-1730, £4.50, concessions £3.60, children £2.70*, was built around 1600 by the notorious Patrick Stewart, Earl of Orkney, using forced labour. Still very much intact, it is one of Scotland's most elegant Renaissance buildings and was occupied by the tyrannical Stewart only for a very short time, until he was imprisoned and later executed. Wandering around both these impressive and solid palaces is a very good way to get a feel for this period of Orkney's history.

Opposite St Magnus Cathedral is **Tankerness House and Gardens**, a 16th-century former manse which has been restored and now houses the **Orkney Museum** ① *T01856-873535, Oct-Apr Mon-Sat 1030-1230, 1330-1700, May-Sep 1030-1700, free*, which highlights 5500 years of human presence on Orkney, including archaeological artefacts from Neolithic times to the Vikings. If you are spending any time in Kirkwall at the beginning of your stay, then this is an exceedingly worthwhile exhibition. It is a great way to whet your appetite for the archaeological treats that are lying in wait for you all over the islands, and it also puts them into a useful chronological context.

Old radio buffs should not miss the **Orkney Wireless Museum** ① *Kiln Corner, at the harbour end of Junction Rd, T01856-871400, www.orkneywirelessmuseum.org.uk, Apr-Sep Mon-Sat 1000-1630, Sun 1430-1630, small entry fee*, which houses a jumble of domestic and wartime communications equipment from the 1930s onwards.

A mile south of the town centre on the road to South Ronaldsay is the 200-year-old **Highland Park Distillery** ① *T01856-874619, www.highlandpark.co.uk, tours on the hour every hour with the last tour 1 hr before closing Apr and Sep Mon-Fri 1000-1700, May-Aug Mon-Sat 1000-1700, Sun 1200-1700, Oct-Mar Mon-Fri 1300-1600, £6*. This is one of the few distilleries that still has its own floor maltings – as well as its own mouser cat – and there's a dram of this particularly fine single malt at the end. Don't leave without buying a bottle, for this is one of the great all-round whiskies, with a distinctive smoky flavour. It rivals those from more fashionable Islay.

Stromness and West Mainland → For listings, see pages 53-62. Phone code 01856.

Ferries from Scrabster arrive in Stromness, and newcomers are greeted by rows of stone-built houses hugging the shore, each with its own jetty. Stromness is a much more attractive town than Kirkwall, and its narrow, winding main street, its *wynds* and *closes*, its fascinating shops and its unique atmosphere make it the ideal base for exploring the West Mainland, the name given to everything west of Kirkwall. It's an area of rich farmland, rolling hills and moorland, fringed by spectacular cliffs along the Atlantic coastline and with the greatest concentration of prehistoric monuments in Britain. Here you'll find, amongst many others, the well-preserved Neolithic village of **Skara Brae**, silent monuments to human endeavour in the form of the **Standing Stones of Stenness** and the **Ring of Brodgar**, and the chambered tomb of **Maes Howe**, with its many still-unresolved mysteries.

Arriving in Stromness and the West Mainland
Getting there and around Northlink Ferries sail from Scrabster to Stromness (1½ hours) three times a day Monday to Friday and twice a day on Saturday and Sunday. Between mid-June and mid-August, they sail three times a day Monday to Saturday. Passenger fare is £19.15 single (child £9.65) and a car costs £58, in peak season. **Rapsons Coaches** (www.rapsons.com), and **Citylink** (www.citylink.co.uk) operate bus services between Thurso and Scrabster and **Stagecoach** operates a daily service from Inverness to Scrabster. There is also a regular train service to Thurso from Inverness.

There are several buses between Kirkwall and Stromness, Monday to Friday, and two buses daily between Kirkwall and Birsay Palace. To get to Skara Brae you'll need your own transport, or you can visit as part of a guided tour (see the TIC), or walk north along the coast from Stromness, via Yesnaby. ▶▶ *For further information, see Transport, page 61.*

Tourist information Stromness TIC ① *T01856-850716, Apr-Oct Mon-Sat 0900-1800, Sun 0900-1600*, is at the ferry terminal. Its exhibition, *This Place Called Orkney*, is a useful introduction to the islands, and its free *Stromness Heritage Guide* takes you round all the town's buildings.

Stromness

Stromness is a classic Scottish fishing town and a perfect introduction to Orkney. Though referred to in the Viking Saga as *Hamnavoe*, the town dates from the 17th century. Its importance as a trading port grew in the 18th century when wars and privateers made the English Channel too dangerous and ships used the northern route across the Atlantic, calling in at Stromness for food and water and to hire a crew. Until the late 19th century, ships of the Hudson Bay Company made Stromness their main base for supplies. Whaling ships bound for Greenland also hired local labour. By the late 19th century the herring boom had reached Stromness and there were 400 boats using its harbour, but within two decades the boom had ended due to over-fishing. Today Stromness remains a fishing port, as well as Orkney's main ferry terminal and the headquarters of the Northern Lighthouse Board.

Stromness consists largely of one narrow, winding main street, paved with flagstones, which hugs the shoreline. Running off the street are numerous little lanes and alleyways, many with names such as **Khyber Pass**, that are full of interesting buildings that reflect the town's proud maritime heritage. The houses on the seaward side of the street are gable end to the waterfront and each has its own jetty. The town is not designed for the car, so you'll have to park by the harbour and explore its delights on foot. The main street changes its name from Victoria Street to Graham Place, Dundas Street, Alfred Street and South End as it runs south from the harbour.

Stromness Museum ① *52 Albert St, T01856-850025, www.orkneyheritage.com, Apr-Sep daily 1000-1700, Oct-Mar Mon-Sat 1100-1530, £3.50, concessions £2.50, children £1, family £7*, run by a community trust, is packed to the gunnels with exhibitions on Stromness' social and maritime history, including the story of Arctic whaling and artefacts from Scapa Flow and the days of the Hudson Bay Company. Upstairs the beautiful Victorian glass cases house a complete collection of Orkney birds and butterflies. Recommended. Opposite the museum is the house where George Mackay Brown (1921-1996), Orkney's most famous poet and story writer, spent the last two decades of his life. On a jetty to the south of the new harbour is the excellent **Pier Arts Centre** ① *T01856-850209, www.pierartscentre.com, Mon-Sat 1030-1730 Sun 1200-1600, free*, housing a permanent collection of works of the St Ives school, including Barbara Hepworth, Ben Nicholson and Patrick Heron, amongst others, in a lovely contemporary gallery.

Skara Brae and Skaill House

① *T01956-841815, www.historic-scotland.gov.uk. Apr-Sep (joint ticket) daily 0930-1730. £7.10, concessions £5.70, children £4.30. Oct-Mar (Skara Brae only) daily 0930-1630, £6.10, concessions £4.90, children £3.70.*

Eight miles north of Stromness, in the magnificent setting of the dazzling white sands of the Bay of Skaill, is Skara Brae, the best-preserved Stone Age village in northern Europe. Explore here and you may feel you have just joined the cartoon world of The Flintstones.

First revealed in 1850 after a violent storm blew away the dunes, this amazing site dates from around 5000 years ago and was occupied for about 600 years.

The houses contain stone furniture, fireplaces, drains, beds, dressers and even have damp-proof coursing in the foundations. The whole complex presents a unique picture of the lifestyle of its inhabitants, and there's also a replica 'house' that you can wander around in the gloom, empathizing with that 3000 BC lifestyle.

The swish, modern visitor centre has a useful introductory video and exhibition which is definitely worth seeing before you look round the site (and it's also worth buying their guidebook). After leaving the visitor centre, you walk down a 'path of time', which takes you back through landmark achievements of the last seven millennia, gradually building up the suspense and putting the achievements of Skara Brae in perspective – they may only be rudimentary buildings that once had turf for their rooves, but they were built 2000 years before the pyramids of Egypt, and in one of the world's most northerly outposts.

During the summer a ticket to Skara Brae includes admission to nearby **Skaill House** ⓘ *T01856-841501, www.skaillhouse.com*, an early 17th-century mansion which contains a few old artefacts, including Captain Cook's dinner service from the *Resolution* and the trappings and frippery of the Lairds of Brackness over 400 years. Seeing these Orcadian dwellings, hundreds of thousands of years apart, is remarkable.

Sandwick and Yesnaby

A short distance inland from here, at Sandwick, is Orkney's only brewery, housed in the old Quoyloo School. It brews the island's **Raven Ale** and various bottled beers, including **Skull-splitter**, named after the Viking earl, Thorfinn Skull-splitter.

South of the Bay of Skaill is Yesnaby, one of the most spectacular places on the islands, where the cliffs have been eroded into a series of stacks and geos by the fierce Atlantic seas. An exhilarating and precarious half-mile walk south from the car park and old Second World War lookout post brings you to **Yesnaby Castle**, a huge sea stack similar to the Old Man of Hoy. It's a dramatic sight, especially in a full force gale.

Markwick Head

North of Skara Brae at the southern end of Birsay Bay are the wild and spectacular 300-ft-high cliffs of Marwick Head, topped by the distinctive **Kitchener Memorial**, erected after the First World War to commemorate Lord Kitchener and the crew of the *HMS Hampshire*, which was sunk by a German mine off the coast in 1916 with the loss of all but 12 of her crew. Marwick Head is also an **RSPB Reserve**, and during the nesting season in early summer is home to many thousands of guillemots, razorbills, kittiwakes and fulmars, as well as a few puffins.

A mile inland, by the Loch of Isbister, is another RSPB reserve, **The Loons**, an area of marshland where you can see breeding and migrating wildfowl and waders. Further east, between Boardhouse Loch and Hundland Loch, is the **Kirbuster Farm Museum** ⓘ *T01856-873535, Mar-Oct Mon-Sat 1030-1300, 1400-1700, Sun 1400-1900, free*, the last surviving Orkney blackhouse which was inhabited till the 1960s and gives an insight into 19th-century rural life on the islands.

Birsay

At the far northwestern corner of the Mainland is the parish of Birsay, which was a favourite residence of the Earls of Orkney in Viking times as well as the first seat of the Bishop, before the building of St Magnus Cathedral in Kirkwall. Earl Thorfinn the Mighty lived here (1014-1064) and built Orkney's first cathedral, **Christchurch**, for the new Bishop.

In the centre of the village are the ruins of the **Earl's Palace** ① *T01856-721205, open at all times, free,* built by the infamous Earl Robert Stewart in the late 16th century, and once described as "a sumptuous and stately dwelling". Not much remains today, but enough to give some idea of the sheer scale of the place. Close by is **St Magnus church**, built in 1760 on the site of an earlier church, which in turn built on the foundations of what is believed to be the original Christchurch. Also in Birsay, just south of the A966 and A967 junction, is **Barony Mills** ① *T01856-721439, www.birsay.org.uk, May-Sep daily 1000-1300, 1400-1700, free,* the last working water-powered mill in Orkney.

Lying half a mile off the coast near the village is the **Brough of Birsay** ① *phone the Earl's Palace (see above) or T01856-841815 for crossing times, open (when tides permit) mid-Jun to end Sep daily 0930-1730, £4.50, concessions £3.60, children £2.70.* The tidal island, managed by Historic Scotland, juts out into the north Atlantic and is visible from several other points all the way down the west coast of the Mainland. It is only accessible for a couple of hours at low tide (times available from Kirkwall and Stromness tourist offices) but, if possible, it is best seen at the end of the day, as the sun sets – you'll probably have the whole island to yourself. Pick your way over the causeway and wander at your leisure (but don't forget the tide) amongst the remnants of a Pictish, and then Viking, community. The island was an important Pictish settlement from around the sixth century, and many artefacts have been found here. Some of these can be seen at the small ticket office at the entrance to the island. The Brough was also the site of an important Viking settlement, and there are extensive remains, including the 12th-century **St Peter's church** where St Magnus was buried after his murder on Egilsay. You can also walk out to the island's lighthouse along the top of the cliffs and see puffins – amongst other migrating seabirds – and possibly minke whales, pilot whales and killer whales.

Evie and the Broch of Gurness

Nine miles northwest of Kirkwall, or 14 miles east of Birsay, is the tiny village of Evie. A track leads from the village towards the coast, past a sandy beach, to the **Broch of Gurness** ① *T01856-751414, Apr-Oct daily 0930-1730, £5.50, concessions £4.40, children £3.30.* Standing on a lonely, exposed headland on the north coast, with gentle views across towards the island of Rousay, this is the best-preserved broch on Orkney, thought to date from around 100 BC. It is surrounded by an Iron Age village whose houses are also remarkably well preserved, with the original hearths, beds, cupboards and even a toilet still in evidence. The broch and village were occupied by the Picts up until Viking times, around AD 900. Many Pictish artefacts have been found on the site, and the grave of a ninth-century Norse woman was also discovered.

To the southwest of Evie is the **Birsay Moors RSPB Reserve**, and at **Lowrie's Water** on Burgar Hill there's a bird-hide from where you can watch breeding red-throated divers. Also on Burgar Hill you'll see several huge aerogenerators built to take advantage of Orkney's fierce winds.

Standing Stones of Stenness and Ring of Brodgar

Northeast of Stromness on the road to Kirkwall is the tiny village of **Stenness**, near some of Orkney's most interesting prehistoric sites. The Standing Stones of Stenness comprise the four remaining stones from an original circle of 12 stones, dating from 3000 BC. The largest of the stones stands over 15 ft high. A path leads from the stones to the nearby **Barnhouse Settlement**, a recently excavated Neolithic village.

About a mile northwest of Stenness is another stone circle, the **Ring of Brodgar**. This is a particularly impressive henge monument. It is over 100 yds in diameter and 27 of the original 60 stones are still standing, some of them up to 15 ft high. Given the importance of these sites, it is particularly refreshing to realize when you get there that you can walk amongst the stones in the calm of a summer evening, with only a few oystercatchers for company, but both get busy with coach parties during the day.

Maes Howe

① *T01856-761606, www.historic-scotland.gov.uk. Apr-Sep daily 0930-1700, Oct-Mar daily 0930-1630, £5.50, concessions £4.40, children £3.30. Tickets can be bought from Tormiston Mill, on the other side of the road, where there's an exhibition, introductory video and café. Tours at 45-min intervals, call to book.*

Less than a mile northeast of the Stones of Stenness is Maes Howe, the finest Neolithic burial chamber in Europe. It was built around 2750 BC, making it contemporary with the Standing Stones and Skara Brae, and is amazingly well preserved. A huge mound covers a stone-built entrance passage which leads into a central chamber – over 12 ft square and the same in height – with three smaller cells built into the walls of the tomb.

When it was opened in 1861, no human remains or artefacts were found, giving no clues as to its usage. However, in the 12th century Vikings returning from the Crusades broke into the tomb searching for treasure. They found nothing, but left behind one of the largest collections of runic graffiti anywhere in the world, as well as carvings of a dragon, serpent and walrus. Many of the inscriptions are pretty basic, along the lines of 'Thorfinn wrote these runes', but some are more intriguing, such as "Many a woman has come stooping in here no matter how pompous a person she was".

A guide gives you an excellent overview of the chamber's mysterious architectural attributes, but the fact remains that the history of this extraordinary place is still largely unsolved – something that obviously adds to the site's attraction. Unfortunately, you do not get to spend much time in the chamber, so you are unlikely to uncover any great secrets.

Orphir

On the southern shores of West Mainland, southeast of Stenness and overlooking Scapa Flow, is the scattered community of Orphir, which has a few sights worth visiting, especially if you're heading across to Hoy from the ferry terminal at **Houton**, a little further west. The main point of interest in Orphir is the **Orkneyinga Saga Centre** ① *T01856-811319, open all year daily 0900-1700, free*, where a small exhibition and video introduces the saga of the Viking Earls of Orkney from around AD 900 to 1200, when the islands became a part of Scotland rather than Norway. It was written circa 1200, possibly by an Icelander. As you would expect, there's plenty of gore and Machiavellian goings-on, including an assassination attempt that went disastrously wrong, when a poisoned shirt meant for Earl Harold was unwittingly and fatally worn by his brother Paul instead.

Behind the centre is **The Earl's Bu**, looking out across Orphir Bay south to Cava Island. These are the 12th-century foundations of the home of the Norse Earls of Orkney written about in the saga. Inside the cemetery gates is a section of the circular church built by Haakon and modelled on the rotunda of the Church of the Holy Sepulchre in Jerusalem.

East Mainland and South Ronaldsay → *For listings, see pages 53-62.*
Phone code 01856.

The East Mainland is mainly agricultural land and though it contains little of the amazing archaeological wealth of its western counterpart, there are some attractive fishing villages, fine coastal walks and many poignant reminders of Orkney's important wartime role. Linked to East Mainland by a series of causeways, South Ronaldsay is the southernmost of the Orkney islands, only six miles from the Scottish mainland across the stormy Pentland Firth, the most dangerous stretch of water in the British Isles.

Arriving in the East Mainland and South Ronaldsay
Getting there John o'Groats Ferries ① *T01955-611353, www.jogferry.co.uk*, run a small passenger ferry from John o'Groats to Burwick on the southern tip of South Ronaldsay twice a day in May and September, four times a day between June and August. The journey takes 40 minutes. **Pentland Ferries** ① *T01856-831226, T01856-611773 (Gill's Bay), www.pentlandferries.co.uk*, sail from Gill's Bay (between John o'Groats and Thurso) to St Margaret's Hope, three times a day (£15 single, children 5-15 £7 (under 5 free), car £35 (not including driver), bicycles free. There are daily buses from Kirkwall to St Margaret's Hope and Burwick on South Ronaldsay.

Deerness
There is not much to see inland on the road running southeast from Kirkwall past the airport, but head on towards the Deerness Peninsula and you will be richly rewarded by a truly serene, gentle beauty. There are sandy bays, which make for very pleasant short walks and picnics (if you can find a sheltered spot), jutting cliffs and a great variety of birdlife. The peninsula makes the West Mainland seem positively crowded by comparison, and is one of the best places on the Mainland to 'get away from it all'.

When the weather's good, the view southwest from Sandside Bay to the Isle of **Copinsay** (an RSPB reserve) is glorious, and is a perfect example of the whale-like properties that have been attributed to the Orkneys by the islands' most famous poet George Mackay Brown. There is a footpath following the coast from Sandside Bay to Mull Head (a nature reserve) and round the tip of the peninsula to the **Covenanters Memorial** (1679), a five-mile circular walk.

If you continue along the B9050, the road ends at The Gloup car park at Skaill Bay, from where it's a 200-yd walk to **The Gloup**, a dramatic collapsed sea cave, separated from the sea by a land bridge about 80 yds wide. The word comes from the Old Norse 'gluppa', meaning chasm, the local name for a blow-hole. A network of signposted footpaths covers the northeastern part of the peninsula and there are circular walks of between two to five miles which start from The Gloup car park. At the northeastern tip is **Mull Head**, a clifftop nature reserve which is home to guillemots, shags, fulmars, razorbills, terns and skuas.

On the south coast of East Mainland, near the northern end of the Churchill Barriers, is the old fishing village of **St Mary's**, once a busy little place but largely forgotten since the building of the causeways. To the east of the village is the **Norwood Museum** ① *T01856-781217, May-Sep Tue-Thu and Sun 1400-1700 or by appointment, £2.50, children £1.75*, which features the large and eclectic antique collection of local stonemason Norris Wood.

The Churchill Barriers
East Mainland is linked to a string of islands to the south by four causeways, known as the Churchill Barriers, built on the orders of Prime Minister Winston Churchill during the Second World War as anti-submarine barriers to protect the British Navy which was based in Scapa Flow at the time. Churchill's decision was prompted by the sinking of the battleship *HMS Royal Oak* in October 1939 by a German U-boat which had slipped between the old blockships, deliberately sunk during the First World War to protect Scapa

The graveyard of Scapa Flow

The huge natural harbour of Scapa Flow has been used since Viking times, and in the years leading up to the First World War the Royal Navy held exercises there, sometimes involving up to 100 ships. But Scapa was vulnerable to attack, and over the course of the war defences were improved with 21 blockships sunk at the eastern approaches. Scapa Flow continued to be used as the main naval base in the Second World War, but the blockships were not enough to prevent a German U-boat from torpedoing *HMS Royal Oak*, and the huge task of building the Churchill Barriers began, see page 44.

Scapa Flow's most famous incident happened at the end of the First World War, when, under the terms of the Armistice, Germany agreed to surrender most of her navy. Seventy-four German ships were interred in Scapa Flow, awaiting the final decision, but as the deadline approached the German commander, Admiral Von Reuter, gave the order for all the ships to be scuttled, and every ship was beached or sunk.

The scuttled German fleet, however, proved a hazard for fishing and a massive salvage operation began. Today seven German ships remain at the bottom of Scapa Flow – three battleships and four light cruisers – along with four destroyers, a U-boat and the Royal Navy battleships *HMS Royal Oak* and *HMS Vanguard*, which blew up in 1917.

Flow, and the shore. After the war, a road was built on top of the causeways, linking the islands of Lamb Holm, Glimps Holm, Burray and South Ronaldsay to Mainland.

On the island of **Lamb Holm** camps were built to accommodate the men working on the construction of the barriers, many of whom were Italian prisoners of war. The camps have long since gone, but the Italians left behind the remarkable **Italian Chapel** ① *T01856-872856 (for mass times), open all year during daylight hours, donations welcomed*, fittingly known as 'The Miracle of Camp 60'. It is difficult to believe that such a beautiful building could have been made using two Nissen huts, concrete and bits of scrap metal, and the chapel's enduring popularity with visitors is a tribute to the artistic skill of the men involved. One of them, Domenico Chiochetti, returned in 1960 to restore the interior paintwork.

Burray

On the island of Burray the road passes the **Orkney Fossil and Vintage Centre** ① *T01856-731255, www.orkneyfossilcentre.co.uk, Apr-Sep daily 1000-1800, Oct Wed-Sun 1030-1800, £4, child/concession £2.50*, which houses a bizarre collection of old furniture, various relics and 350 million-year-old fish fossils found locally. There's also an archive room where you can browse old books and photographs. Not really something to go out of your way for, but worth a look if it's raining.

South Ronaldsay

The main settlement is the picturesque little village of **St Margaret's Hope** on the north coast. It is said to be named after Margaret, Maid of Norway, who died near here in 1290 at the age of seven while on her way to marry Prince Edward, later Edward II of England. She had already been proclaimed Queen of Scotland, and her premature death was a major factor in the long Wars of Independence with England. The word 'hope' comes from the Old Norse word *hjop* meaning bay.

The village smithy has been turned into the **Smiddy Museum** ① *T01856-831567, May and Sep daily 1400-1600, Jun-Aug daily 1200-1600, Oct Sun 1400-1600, free,* with lots of old blacksmith's tools to try out. The museum also features a small exhibition on the annual **Boys' Ploughing Match**, a hugely popular event first held circa 1860. Each year in August, boys from the village (and now girls as well) dress up as horses and parade in the village square (prizes are given for the best costume). Afterwards the boys and their fathers, or grandfathers, head for the **Sand of Wright**, a few miles west, and have a ploughing match with miniature ploughs, which are usually family heirlooms. The categories are: best ploughed ring, best feering or guiding furrow, neatest ends and best-kept plough. This sheltered beach is well worth a visit anyway, ploughing or no ploughing. The views stretch in a spectacular 180° panorama, south across the Pentland Firth to Caithness on mainland Scotland, west to South Walls and Cantick Head on Hoy, and northwest to Flotta and the west Mainland. It is yet another good place to spot snipe, lapwing, curlew and redshank. Arctic terns nest nearby and you can spot them diving dramatically as they fish in the bay.

To the north of the beach is the **Howe of Hoxa**, a ruined broch where Earl Thorfinn Skull-Splitter was buried in AD 963, according to the Orkneyinga saga. South Ronaldsay is a good place to buy local arts and crafts, and there are several workshops dotted around the island. One of these is the **Hoxa Tapestry Gallery** ① *T01856-831395, www.hoxatapestrygallery.co.uk,* three miles west of the village on the way to Hoxa Head. Local artist Leila Thompson's huge tapestries are well worth a visit; you cannot help but marvel at the extraordinary amount of work and dedication involved in their creation; many of them take years to finish. Due to the success of the gallery, Leila Thompson now works mostly to commission with lengthy waiting times.

At the southeastern corner of South Ronaldsay is the **Tomb of the Eagles** ① *T01856-831339, www.tomboftheeagles.co.uk, Mar daily 1000-1200, Apr-Sep daily 0930-1730, Oct 0930-1230, Nov-Feb by arrangement, £7, concessions £6, children 13+ £3,* children 5-12 £2, one of the most interesting archaeological sights on Orkney. The 5000-year-old chambered cairn was discovered by local farmer and amateur archaeologist, Ronald Simison, whose family now runs the privately owned site and museum. The contents of the tomb were practically intact and there were up to 340 people buried here, along with carcasses and talons of sea eagles, hence the name. Various objects were also found outside the tomb, including stone tools and axes.

Before visiting the tomb you can handle the skulls and other artefacts at the small 'museum' in the family home, which actually means their front porch. Then you walk for about five or 10 minutes through a field to visit a **burnt mound**, a kind of Bronze Age kitchen, where – if you're lucky – Ronald Simison will regail you with insider information about the excavation process, before walking out along the cliff edge to the spectacularly sited tomb which you must enter by lying on a trolley and pulling yourself in using an overhead rope. It is particularly eerie being here because there is generally no-one else around, and as you haul yourself into the tomb, with the sound of the North Sea crashing into the cliffs nearby, you wonder to yourself how those buried here met their fate. There is also a lovely, but generally wild and windy, walk back along the cliffs, via a different route, to the car park.

In South Ronaldsay too is the **Orkney Marine-Life Aquarium** ① *Pool Farmhouse, Grimness, T01856-831700, www.orkneymarinelife.co.uk, daily 1000-1800, £6, concession £5, children 3-15 £4.25,* that as the name suggests offers visitors of all ages an insight to the creatures of the deep around these shores. Year round, it's well worth a visit.

Hoy → *For listings, see pages 53-62. Phone code 01856.*

To the southwest of the Mainland is Hoy, the second largest of the Orkney islands. The name is derived from the Norse *Ha-ey*, meaning High Island, which is appropriate as much of the island is more reminiscent of the Scottish Highlands than Orkney, with only the southern end being typically low and fertile.

Arriving in Hoy

Getting there and around There are two ferry services to Hoy, both run by **Orkney Ferries** ① *T01856-872044, www.orkneyferries.co.uk*. A passenger ferry sails between Stromness and Moaness Pier in the north (30 minutes) three times a day from Monday to Friday, twice on Friday evenings, and twice a day on Saturday and Sunday. There's a reduced winter service from mid-September to mid-May. There's also a car and passenger service (T01856-811397) between Houton and Lyness and Longhope (45 minutes) up to six times daily, Monday to Saturday. There's a limited Sunday service from mid-May to mid-September.

Transport on Hoy is very limited, **North Hoy Transport** ① *T01856-791315*, runs a minibus service between Moaness Pier and Rackwick, which meets the 1000 ferry from Stromness. Call the same telephone number for a taxi around the island. From May to September the Hoy Hopper, T01856-872044, departs from Kirkwall at 0840 and stops at all the sites for just long enough to see them before returning you to Kirkwall (for 1820), £17, child/concession £8.50. There are shops and petrol stations in Lyness and Longhope.
▶▶ *For further details, see Transport, page 61.*

Places in Hoy

Orkney's highest point, **Ward Hill** (1571 ft) is in the north of the island, and the north and west coasts are bounded by spectacular cliffs. At **St John's Head**, the sheer cliffs rise out of the sea to a height of 1150 ft, the highest vertical cliffs in Britain. The island is most famous for its **Old Man of Hoy**, a great rock stack rising to 450 ft. This northern part of Hoy forms the **North Hoy RSPB Reserve** which has a variety of habitats ranging from woodland to tundra-like hilltops and sea cliffs. The reserve is home to a huge variety of birds including great skuas and Arctic skuas, Manx shearwaters and puffins. On the hills there are red grouse, curlews, golden plovers and dunlins, peregrine falcons, merlins, kestrels and even golden eagles. Mountain hares are quite common and, if you are lucky, you can also see otters along the Scapa Flow coastline.

On the southeast coast of the island is **Lyness**, site of a large naval base during both world wars when the British fleet was based in Scapa Flow. Many of the old dilapidated buildings have gone, but the harbour area is still scarred with the scattered remains of concrete structures, and there's also the unattractive sight of the huge oil terminal on **Flotta**. Lyness has a large **Naval Cemetery**, last resting place of those who died at Jutland, of Germans killed during the scuttle and of the crew of *HMS Royal Oak*. The old pump house opposite the new ferry terminal is now the **Scapa Flow Visitor Centre** ① *T01856-791300, mid-May to Sep Mon-Fri 0900-1630, Sat-Sun 1000-1600, free*, a fascinating naval museum with old photographs, various wartime artefacts, a section devoted to the scuttling of the German fleet and an audio-visual feature on the history of Scapa Flow. It's well worth a visit and is reached by a short ferry trip across Scapa Flow. At South Walls, overlooking Longhope Bay, is **Hackness Martello Tower and Battery** ① *T01856-811397 (HS), Apr-Oct daily 0930-1730, Oct 0930-1730, £4.50, concessions £3.60, children £2.70*, which, along with another tower on the north side at Crockness, was built in 1815 to protect British ships in

Longhope Bay against attack by American and French privateers while they waited for a Royal Navy escort on their journey to Baltic ports.

Walking on Hoy

Hoy's great attraction is its many excellent walking opportunities. A minibus runs between **Moaness Pier**, where the ferry from Stromness docks (see Transport, page 61), and **Rackwick**, on the opposite side of the island, but it's a lovely two-hour walk by road through beautiful **Rackwick Glen**, once populated by crofters and fishermen, but now quiet and isolated. On the way you'll pass the **Dwarfie Stone**, a huge, lonely block of sandstone which is the only rock-cut tomb in Britain, dating from around 3000 BC. Be careful, though, because, according to Sir Walter Scott, this is the residence of the Trolld, a dwarf from Norse legend. On your return you can take a different route through a narrow valley between the **Cuilags** (1421 ft) and **Ward Hill** and **Berriedale Wood**, the most northerly woodland in Britain. The most popular walk on Hoy is the spectacular three-hour hike from Rackwick to the cliffs facing the **Old Man of Hoy**. The path climbs steeply westwards from the old crofting township, then turns northwards before gradually descending to the cliff edge.

Rousay, Egilsay and Wyre → For listings, see pages 53-62.

These three islands lie a short distance off the northeast coast of Mainland and, together with Shapinsay to the southeast, are the closest of Orkney's North Isles to Kirkwall.

Arriving in Rousay, Egilsay and Wyre

Getting there A small car ferry operated by **Orkney Ferries** sails from Tingwall to Rousay up to six times a day Monday to Saturday, and five times a day on Sunday. Most of the ferries call in at Egilsay and Wyre, but some are on demand only and should be booked in advance, T01856-872044. ▸▸ For further information, see Transport, page 61.

Rousay

Rousay is a hilly island about five miles in diameter and is known as the 'Egypt of the North' due to the large number of archaeological sites. It also has the important **Trumland RSPB Reserve**, home to merlins, hen harriers, peregrine falcons, short-eared owls and red-throated divers, and its three lochs offer good trout fishing.

A road runs right around the island, and makes a pleasant 13-mile bike run, but most of the sights are within walking distance of the ferry pier on the southeast side of the island, where most of the 200 inhabitants live. A short distance west of the pier by the road is **Tavershoe Tuick**, an unusual two-storey burial cairn, which was discovered in the late 19th century by Mrs Burroughs, wife of General Traill Burroughs who lived at nearby Trumland House. A mile further west, to the north of the road, is **Blackhammer**, a stalled Neolithic burial cairn. Further west still, and a steep climb up from the road, is **Knowe of Yarso**, another stalled cairn, which contained the remains of at least 21 people. The tomb dates from around 2900 BC.

Most of the island's archaeological sights are to be found along the **Westness Walk**, a mile-long walk which starts from Westness Farm, about four miles west of the ferry pier, and ends at the remarkable Midhowe Cairn. The walk is described in detail in a leaflet available from the tourist offices on Mainland. **Midhowe Cairn** is the largest and longest cairn – over 100 ft long and 40 ft wide – excavated on Orkney thus far and, like the others, dates from around 3000 BC. Housed in a large building to protect it, the 'Great Ship of Death', as it is known, contained the remains of 25 people in crouched position on or under the eastern shelves of the chamber, which is divided into 12 sections. Standing nearby, with fine views across to Eynehallow island, is **Midhowe Broch**, one of the best-preserved brochs on Orkney, occupied from around 200 BC to AD 200. The outer walls are about 60 ft in diameter and up to 14 ft high in places.

Another fine walk on the island is around the **RSPB Reserve**. A footpath leads from beside Trumland House and heads up towards the island's highest point, **Blotchnie Field** (821 ft). A leaflet describing the walk is available from the tourist offices on Mainland or the **Trumland Orientation Centre** by the pier.

Egilsay and Wyre

These two small islands lie to the east of Rousay and have a couple of interesting sights of their own. Egilsay's claim to fame is the murder here of St Magnus in 1115, and a **cenotaph** marks the spot where he was slain. The island is dominated by the 12th-century **St Magnus church**, built on the site of an earlier church, possibly as a shrine to St Magnus. It is the only surviving example on Orkney of a round-towered Viking church. Much of Egilsay has been bought by the RSPB as a reserve to preserve the habitat of the very rare **corncrake**, whose distinctive rasping call may be heard.

Tiny Wyre features strongly in the Viking saga as the domain of Kolbein Hruga, and the remains of his 12th-century stronghold, **Cubbie Roo's Castle**, and nearby **St Mary's chapel** can be still be seen. Kolbein's home was on the site of the nearby Bu Farm, where the poet Edwin Muir (1887-1959) spent part of his childhood. The far westerly point of the island, known as **the Taing**, is a favourite haunt of seals, and a great place to enjoy a sunset.

Shapinsay → *For listings, see pages 53-62. Phone code 01856.*

Less than 30 minutes by ferry from Kirkwall is the fertile, low-lying island of Shapinsay, home to **Balfour Castle** ① *T01856-711282, www.balfourcastle.co.uk*, an imposing baronial pile which is in fact a Victorian extension to a much older house called 'Cliffdale'. The house, and the rest of the island, was bought by successive generations of the Balfour family who had made their fortune in India. Today the castle is the home of the Zawadski family and is rented to small house parties (see Where to stay, page 55). The castle can also be visited as part of a half-day tour, which leaves from Kirkwall on Sundays in August. Arrange in advance at the tourist office in Kirkwall. The ticket includes a guided tour of the castle and gardens (at 1500) and complimentary tea and cakes in the servants' quarters. You can also take an earlier ferry if you wish to explore the island. The small car ferry makes up to six sailings daily (including Sunday in summer) to Shapinsay from Kirkwall (25 minutes).

In the village, built by the Balfours to house their estate workers, is the **Shapinsay Heritage Centre** ① *T01856-711258, open daily May-Sep, free*, in the old Smithy. It has displays on the island's history and a tea room upstairs. There's a **pub** in the village, in the old gatehouse, a couple of shops and a post office.

A mile north of the village is the **Mill Dam RSPB Reserve**, where there's a hide overlooking a loch from which you can see many species of wildfowl and waders. Four miles from the pier, at the far northeast corner of the island, is the well-preserved **Burroughston Broch**, with good views of seals sunning themselves on the nearby rocks. West of here, at **Quholme**, is the original birthplace of the father of Washington Irving, author of *Rip Van Winkle*.

Eday → *For listings, see pages 53-62. Phone code 01857.*

The long, thin and sparsely populated island of Eday lies at the centre of the North Isles group. It is less fertile than the other islands, but its heather-covered hills in the centre have provided peat for the other peatless Orkney islands. Eday's sandstone has also been quarried, and was used in the building of St Magnus Cathedral in Kirkwall.

Arriving in Eday

There are flights from Kirkwall to Eday airport, called London Airport, on Wednesdays with **Loganair** ① *T01856-872494*. There are ferries also from Kirkwall twice daily via Sanday or Stronsay. Note that the pier is at Backaland, on the southeast of the island, a long way from the main sights. **Orkney Ferries** ① *T01856-872044*, also run the Eday Heritage Tour (see page 59). ▶▶ *For further details, see Transport, page 61.*

Places in Eday

The island has numerous chambered cairns and these, along with the other attractions, are concentrated in the northern part. They are all covered in the signposted five-mile **Eday Heritage Walk**, which starts from the Community Centre and leads up to the cliffs of Red Head at the northern tip. The walk takes about four hours to complete, and it's worth picking up the *Eday Heritage Walk* leaflet.

The walk heads past **Mill Loch**, where an RSPB hide allows you to watch rare red-throated divers breeding in spring and summer. Further north is the huge, 15-ft tall **Stone of Setter**, the largest standing stone in Orkney and visible from most of the chambered cairns. Close by are the **Fold of Setter**, a circular enclosure dating back to 2000 BC, and the **Braeside** and **Huntersquoy** chambered cairns. Further north along the path is **Vinquoy Chambered Cairn**, one of the finest in Orkney and similar to the better-known tomb at Maes Howe, dating from around the same time. An acrylic dome provides light to the main chamber, which can be entered by a narrow underground passage.

The path continues to the summit of **Vinquoy Hill**, which commands excellent views of the surrounding islands of Westray and Sanday. From here you can continue north to the spectacular red sandstone cliffs at **Red Head**, home to nesting guillemots, razorbills and puffins in summer, or head southeast along the coast to **Carrick House** ① *T01857-622260, guided tour mid-Jun to mid-Sep, Sun by appointment, free, donations to charity only*. Built for Lord Kinclaven, Earl of Carrick, in 1633, the house is best known for its associations with the pirate, John Gow, whose ship ran aground during a failed attack on the house. He was captured and taken to London for trial and hanged. Sir Walter Scott's novel, *The Pirate*, is based on this story.

Sanday → *For listings, see pages 53-62. Phone code 01857.*

Sanday is the largest of the North Isles, 12 miles long and flat as a pancake except for the cliffs at Spurness. It is well-named, as its most notable feature is its sweeping bays of sparkling white sand backed by machair and fronted by turquoise seas. There are **Loganair** flights to Sanday from Kirkwall twice daily from Monday to Friday and once a day on Saturday. Ferries run twice daily from Kirkwall (1½ hours) and arrive at Loth, at the southern tip of the island, where they're met by a minibus.

There are numerous burial mounds all over the island, the most impressive being **Quoyness Chambered Cairn**, a 5000 year-old tomb similar to Maes Howe. The 13 ft-high structure contains a large main chamber with six smaller cells opening through low entrances. Most of the burial tombs remain unexcavated, such as those at **Tofts Ness** at the far northeastern tip, where there are over 500 cairns, making it potentially one of the most important prehistoric sites in Britain. At **Scar**, in Burness, a spectacular Viking find was made, and at **Pool** a major excavation has uncovered the remains of at least 14 Stone-Age houses.

Sanday is known for its knitwear, though the factory unfortunately closed down. You can still visit the **Orkney Angora craft shop**, in Upper Breckan, near the northern tip of the island.

Stronsay → *For listings, see pages 53-62.*

Arriving in Stronsay → *Phone code 01857.*
Getting there There are **Loganair** flights from Kirkwall twice daily from Monday to Friday. A ferry service runs from Kirkwall twice daily Monday to Saturday and once on Sunday (1½ hours), and the ferry from Eday runs once a day from Monday to Saturday (35 minutes).

Places in Stronsay
The peaceful, low-lying island of Stronsay has some fine sandy beaches and cliffs, which attract large colonies of grey seals and nesting seabirds. There are few real sights on this largely agricultural island, but the coastline has some pleasant walks. One of the best is to the **Vat of Kirbister** in the southeast, a spectacular 'gloup' or blow-hole spanned by the finest natural arch in Orkney. To the south of here, at **Burgh Head**, you'll find nesting puffins and the remains of a ruined broch, and at the southeastern tip, at **Lamb Head**, is a large colony of grey seals, lots of seabirds and several archaeological sites.

The main settlement is the quiet village of **Whitehall**, on the northeast coast where the ferry arrives. It's hard to believe it now, but this was one of the largest herring ports in Europe. During the boom years of the early 20th century, 300 steam drifters were working out of Whitehall and nearly 4000 fishing crew and shore workers were employed. In the peak year of 1924 over 12,000 tons of herring were landed here, to be cured (salted) and exported to Russia and Eastern Europe. Whitehall developed considerably and the **Stronsay Hotel** was said to have the longest bar in Scotland. On Sundays during July and August there were so many boats tied up that it was possible to walk across them to the little island of Papa Stronsay. By the 1930s, however, herring stocks were severely depleted and the industry was in decline. The old Fish Mart by the pier houses a **Heritage Centre** ① *T017856-616386, May-Sep daily 1100-1700, free*, with photos and artefacts from the herring boom days. It also has a café and hostel.

Westray → *For listings, see pages 53-62. Phone code 01857.*

Westray is the second largest of the North Isles, with a varied landscape of farmland, hilly moorland, sandy beaches and dramatic cliffs. It is also the most prosperous of the North Isles, producing beef, fish and seafood, and supports a population of 700. Flights to Westray with Loganair depart Kirkwall twice daily from Monday to Saturday and there's a car ferry service to Rapness, on the south coast of the island (1½ hours). It sails twice daily in summer (mid-May to mid-September) and once daily in winter.

The main settlement is **Pierowall**, in the north of the island, but, though it has one of the best harbours in Orkney, the main ferry terminal is at Rapness, on the south coast. Pierowall is a relatively large village for the North Isles and there are shops, a post office, a hotel and the **Westray Heritage Centre** ① *T01857-677414, www.westrayheritage.co.uk, early May-late Sep Mon 1130-1700, Tue-Sat 1000-1200, 1400-1700, Sun 1330-1700, £2.50, concessions £2, children 50p*, with displays on local and natural history, and a tea room. Also in the village is the ruined 17th-century St Mary's church. About a mile west of the village is Westray's most notable ruin, **Noltland Castle**, a fine example of a 16th-century fortified Z-plan tower-house. To explore inside, pick up the key from the back door of the nearby farm.

Walks on Westray

There are some great coastal walks on the island, particularly to the spectacular sea cliffs at **Noup Head**, at the far northwestern tip, which are an **RSPB Reserve** and second only to St Kilda in terms of breeding seabirds, with huge colonies of guillemots, razorbills, kittiwakes and fulmars, as well as puffins. The cliffs on the west coast of Westray are five miles long and there's an excellent walk down the coast from Noup Head, past **Gentleman's Cave**, used as a hiding place by four Jacobite lairds in 1746. Near the southern end of the walk is **Fitty Hill** (554 ft), the highest point on the island, which you can climb for great views, and the walk ends at **Inga Ness**, where you can also see puffins. The best place to see them is at **Castle o'Burrian**, a sea stack on **Stanger Head**, on the southeastern coast near the Rapness ferry terminal.

Papa Westray → *For listings, see pages 53-62. Phone code 01857.*

Tiny Papa Westray, known locally as 'Papay', is best known as being the destination for the world's shortest scheduled flight, from Westray; it takes all of two minutes, or less with a good following wind, and there's no shortage of that. The famous two-minute flight leaves Westray twice daily (Monday to Saturday). There is also a direct flight to Papay from Kirkwall, daily Monday to Saturday. There's a passenger ferry from Pierowall on Westray three to six times a day, and the car ferry from Kirkwall to Westray continues to Papa Westray on Tuesdays and Fridays (two hours and 15 minutes).

But there are other reasons to visit this little island, one of the most remote of the Orkney group. Papay is home to Europe's oldest house, the **Knap of Howar** ① *open at all times, free*, which was built around 5500 years ago and is still standing (they knew how to build 'em in those days). It's on the west coast, just south of the airport. Half a mile north is **St Boniface Kirk**, one of the oldest Christian sites in the north of Scotland, founded in the eighth century, though most of the recently restored building dates from the 12th century. Inland from the Knap of Howar is **Holland Farm**, former home of the lairds of the island, where you can rummage around the farm buildings and museum.

Papay is famous for its birds, and **North Hill**, on the north of the island, is an important RSPB Reserve. The cliffs are home to many thousands of breeding seabirds, and at **Fowl Craig** on the east coast you can see nesting puffins. The interior is home to the largest arctic tern colony in Europe, as well as many arctic skuas. If you wish to explore you have to contact the warden at **Rose Cottage** ① *T01857-644240*, who runs regular guided walks.

It's worth taking a boat trip to the even tinier, deserted **Holm of Papay**, off the east coast. This is the site of several Neolithic burial cairns, including one of the largest chambered cairns on Orkney. You enter the tomb down a ladder into the main chamber which is nearly 70 ft long, with a dozen side-cells. For boat trips between May and September, call T0776-4569790.

North Ronaldsay → For listings, see pages 53-62.

Remote and storm-battered, North Ronaldsay is the most northerly of the Orkney islands and a place where old Orcadian traditions remain. It seems remarkable that anyone should live here at all in these extreme conditions, but 'North Ron' – as it is known locally – has been inhabited for many centuries and continues to be heavily farmed. The island's sheep are a hardy lot and live exclusively off the seaweed on a narrow strip of beach, outside a 13-mile stone dyke which surrounds the island. This gives their meat a unique, 'gamey' flavour.

This small, flat island, only three miles long, has few real attractions, except to keen ornithologists who flock here to catch a glimpse of its rare migrants. From late March to early June, and mid-August to early November there are huge numbers of migratory birds. The **Bird Observatory**, in the southwest corner of the island by the ferry pier, gives information on which species have been sighted, as well as providing accommodation. There are also colonies of grey seals and cormorants at **Seal Skerry**, on the northeast tip of the island. There are **Loganair** flights from Kirkwall, twice daily from Monday to Saturday and there's a car and passenger ferry which sails from Kirkwall twice a week (usually Tuesday and Friday). Contact **Orkney Ferries** for details.

Orkney listings

For hotel and restaurant price codes and other relevant information, see pages 13-19.

○ Where to stay

Kirkwall *p36, map p37*
There are plenty of good value B&Bs, though don't always expect en suite.
£££ Albert Hotel, Mounthoolie Lane, T01856-87600, www.alberthotel.co.uk. This old Kirkwall hotel has been revamped mixing modern (stylish rooms) with traditional (the cosy Bothy Bar).
£££ Ayre Hotel, Ayre Rd, T01856-873001, www.ayrehotel.co.uk. Open all year. 33 en suite rooms. Kirkwall's most upmarket hotel sits right on the harbour front. Very comfortable with a good restaurant and a bar.
£££ Foveran Hotel, 2 miles from town on the A964 Orphir road at St Ola, T01856-872389, www.foveranhotel.co.uk. Open all year. 8 en suite rooms. Modern, chalet-style hotel overlooking Scapa Flow. Friendly and comfortable, it's renowned for its food (**£££-££**), including scallops, beef and lamb. Food critics have praised the Foveran fudge and cheesecake. Definitely worth a bite.

£££ Kirkwall Hotel, Harbour St, T01856-872232, www.kirkwallhotel.com. Open all year. 37 en suite rooms. Large, imposing building overlooking the harbour. Rooms are reasonably comfortable, service is friendly and efficient, and the restaurant serves good food.
£££ Orkney Hotel, 40 Victoria St, T01856-873477. Whilst investing in an upgrade of its comfortable 30 bedrooms, some with jacuzzi baths and 4-poster beds, the hotel has retained the charm and period features of a dwelling that dates back to 1670. Its **Victoria Restaurant** is also pleasant and good value.
£££ West End Hotel, Main St, T01856-872368, www.westendkirkwall.co.uk. The former house of an old sea captain, this is just along from the cathedral. Has a great restaurant and nicely done rooms.
£ Kirkwall Youth Hostel, Old Scapa Rd, T01856-872243, www.syha.co.uk. Mar-Oct. Large SYHA youth hostel (60 beds) about 15 mins' walk from the town centre.
£ Peedie Hostel, Ayre Rd, T01856-875477, kirkwallpeediehostel@talk21.com. A smaller and more intimate alternative to the SYHA hostel. 11 beds and on the waterfront.

Camping

Pickaquoy Caravan & Camping Site, on the western outskirts of Kirkwall, off the A965, T01856-879900. Apr-Sep. £10.50 for a pitch.

Stromness and West Mainland *p39*

£££ Merkister Hotel, on the shores of Loch Harray, Stenness, T01856-771366, www.merkister.com. 16 rooms, including 3 terraced garden suites. A favourite with anglers, but also handy for archaeological sites, this place has a great location, an excellent restaurant (**££££-£££**) and a popular bar. **££££** for dinner B&B. Deals out of season. One of the best in Orkney. Recommended.

£££ Stromness Hotel, Pier Head, Stromness, T01856-850298, www.stromnesshotel.com. Open all year. 42 en suite rooms. The best hotel in town is this imposing old building overlooking the harbour. Good-value meals.

££ Barony Hotel, Marwick Head, Birsay, T01856-721327, www.baronyhotel.com. May-Sep. 10 rooms. On the north shore of Boardhouse Loch, this small hotel specializes in fishing holidays and is about the only place offering food around here. Central to main bird life sanctuaries and archaeological sites.

££ Mill of Eyreland, Stenness, 3 miles from Stromness, T01856-850136, www.millofeyreland.co.uk. 3 rooms in a lovely converted mill with maintained workings.

££ Netherstove, Sandwick, T01856-841625, www.netherstove.com. May-Oct. 2 rooms. Neat B&B near Skara Brae, overlooking the Bay of Skaill, run by the delightfully named Mrs Poke. Also has 2 self-catering chalets and a cottage (available all year).

££-£ Orca Hotel, Victoria St, near the harbour, Stromness, T01856-850447, www.orcahotel.com. Open all year. 7 en suite rooms. Clean and tidy rooms in this small hotel. Good self-catering deals available Nov-Mar. **£** for room only. Also has a cellar bistro, Bistro 76, serving good food.

££-£ Mrs Sinclair, 45 John St, Stromness, T01856-850949. Close to the ferry, this 2-bedroom B&B serves fortifying breakfasts and will do packed lunches (with home baking).

££-£ Primrose Cottage, Marwick Head, Birsay, T01856-721384. 2 en suite rooms. Comfortable B&B overlooking Marwick Bay. Evening meal and vegetarian options available.

£ Brown's Hostel, 45 Victoria St, Stromness, T01856-850661, www.brownshostel.co.uk. 14 beds. This popular independent hostel has no curfew and is open all year round.

£ Hamnavoe Hostel, 10a North End Rd, Stromness, T01856-851202, www.hamnavoehostel.co.uk. 12 beds. Private, family, twin and single rooms. Recommended.

Self-catering

Eviedale Centre, beside the junction of the road to Dounby, T01856-751254/751270, www.eviedale-orkney.co.uk. Apr-Oct. Has accommodation in a former workshop, barn and stable, from £350 per week) and a campsite.

Woodwick House, Evie, T01856-751330, www.woodwickhouse.co.uk. 8 rooms, 4 en suite. Lovely, old country house in beautiful surroundings. Perfect peace, walks through woods and views across to the islands. From £1500 per week.

Camping

Ness Point, 1 mile south of the ferry terminal, T01856-873535. May to mid-Sep. A well-equipped campsite with incomparable views, but is very exposed.

East Mainland and South Ronaldsay *p43*

There's a good selection of accommodation in St Margaret's Hope.

£££ Creel Restaurant & Rooms, Front Rd, St Margaret's Hope, T01856-831311, www.thecreel.co.uk. 3 en suite rooms. Offers comfortable rooms and delicious food drawn primarily from the day's catch. £40 a head for 3-course dinner only. Also have self-catering apartment fort rent (£60 per night) plus £15 a head for breakfast. Good choice.

£££-££ Eastward Guest House, St Margaret's Hope, T01856-831551, www.eastwardhouse.com. The accommodation in this converted kirk is smart but it's the food in the Missing Bell restaurant made by owner Keiko that's the draw. Her Japanese buffet makes the most of Orkney's seafood (**££££-£££** with dinner). Recommended.

££-£ Commodore Chalets, St Mary's, Holm, T01856-781319, www.commodorechalets.co.uk. This place looks like an army barracks but offers good-value accommodation in nine self-catering chalets and 6 overnight lodges. Good location, with views of Churchill Barriers and within walking distance of Italian Chapel. Price is for B&B. For self-catering, large chalet (sleeps 4-6) is £215-325 per week and small chalet (sleeps 2-4) is £160-260 per week.

££-£ St Margaret's Cottage B&B, South Ronaldsay, T01856-831637, www.stmargaretscottage.com. 3 rooms. Comfortable B&B offering early breakfast option for guests using the Pentland Ferries. Good value.

£ Wheems Organic Farm, Wheems, Eastside, a few miles southeast of St Margaret's Hope, T01856-831556, www.wheemsorganic.co.uk. Apr-Oct. Organic farm offering wooden camping bothies (2.69 m X 1.98 m) which sleep 2 adults. Compact and bijou but wonderful sea views from the front doors. Camping also available.

Hoy *p47*
There's not much accommodation in the north of the island, except for the 2 SYHA hostels. There are a few very good B&Bs in the south.

££ Stromabank Hotel, Longhope, T01856-701494, www.stromabank.co.uk. 4 rooms. Great views across to Orkney and the Scottish mainland. Also serves evening meals to residents and the public during the summer months (phone to book). Meals served Sat-Sun only in winter.

££-£ Quoydale, 1 mile from ferry, T01856-791315, www.orkneyaccommodation.co.uk. B&B in self-contained en-suite room on working farm. Also 2-bed self-catering cottage for £200-350 per week. Taxis, tours and evening meals available.

£ Hoy Centre, about 1 mile from Moaness Pier, T01856-876327, 873535, www.Hostel-scotland.co.uk. May-Sep. Refurbished hostel sleeping 32 in 8 rooms. Family room also available and groups catered for. Book ahead.

£ Rackwick Outdoor Centre, Rackwick Glen, north Hoy, T01856-873535 www.hostelsorkney.co.uk. Mid-Mar to mid-Sep. 8 beds, book ahead.

Rousay, Egilsay and Wyre *p48*
Accommodation is very limited on Rousay, and non-existent on Egilsay and Wyre.

££ Taversoe Hotel, near Knowe of Yarso, about 2 miles west of the pier, T01857-821325, www.taversoehotel.co.uk. 3 rooms with lovely views over Eynhallow Sound. Offers excellent-value meals, the seafood is particularly recommended. Restaurant closed Mon to non-residents. Bar stocks local ales. Transport available to/from the pier.

£ Rousay Hostel, half a mile from the ferry, Trumland Organic Farm, T01856-821252, www.hostel-scotland.co.uk. Open all year. Accommodation for 13. Laundry facilities and camping available. Bikes for hire.

Shapinsay *p49*
££££ Balfour Castle, T01857-711282, www.balfourcastle.com. Live the life of a would-be aristo in this impressive baronial Victorian mansion, set in 70 acres of wooded grounds and still part-family home. The castle has a private chapel and a boat is available for birdwatching and fishing trips for residents, as well as golf, shooting and walking. Also cookery lessons are available with the castle's acclaimed French chef, who

also will prepare his 7-course taster menu for visitors (**£££**). This exclusive retreat does not come cheap: prices start at £2,700 per day all inclusive for 6 guests.

££ Hilton Farm House, T01857-711239, www.hiltonorkneyfarmhouse.co.uk. 3 rooms. Very comfortable B&B, which offers evening meals as well as transport and fishing tours.

Eday p50

£££ Sui Generis, Redbanks, 2 mins' walk from ferry, T01857-622219, www.suigenerisfurniture.co.uk. Beautiful guesthouse/furniture maker. The 2 en suite rooms are truly imaginative and unlike anything else in this part of the world. 3-course dinner, £20. Recommended.

£ Blett, Carrick Bay, opposite the Calf of Eday, T01857-622248. 2 rooms. Very friendly. Evening meal and packed lunch provided if you wish. Mrs Poppelwell also has a self-catering cottage for up to 3 nearby.

£ Youth Hostel, London Bay, T01857-622206. Open all year. Run by Eday Community Enterprises, just north of the airport. Basic lodging but recently refurbished.

Sanday p50

££ The Belsair, Kettletoft, T01857-600206, www.belsairsanday.co.uk. 3 rooms. Large house overlooking the old harbour. Meals served in the bar and dining room, packed lunches available on request. Undergoing renovation at the time of writing.

££ Kettletoft Hotel, Kettletoft, T01857-600217, www.kettletofthotel.com. Most rooms are en suite and are clean, though simply furnished. Serves meals using local produce and has a lively bar. Fish and chip takeaways available on Wed and Sat.

££-£ Backaskaill B&B, Backaskaill, T01857-600298, www.backaskaill.co.uk. Open all year. Friendly and welcoming B&B housed in a Victorian property with a cosy woodburning stove in the lounge. Self-catering evening meals on request.

£ Ayre's Rock Hostel, Ayre, T01857-600410, www.ayres-rock-sanday-orkney.co.uk. Good

facilities but only 7 beds. En suite family room sleeps 4. Also a campsite (£8 per pitch) and 'Pods' sleeping 2 for £20, plus a chip shop takeaway service available on Tue and Sat evenings.

Stronsay p51

££ Stronsay Bird Reserve, Mill Bay, south of Whitehall, T01857-616363. B&B and full-board options available or you can camp overlooking the wide sandy bay.

££ Stronsay Hotel, near the ferry terminal, T01857-616213, www.stronsayhotelorkney.co.uk. Offers 3 doubles and 1 family room, all en suite. Cheap bar food available. Operates as the island's hotel, restaurant and pub.

£ Stronsay Fish Mart Hostel, next to ferry terminal, T01857-616386. Open all year. Well-equipped and comfortable and only a mins' walk from the ferry, see page 51. 3 bedrooms with bunk beds to sleep 10. Their café does cheap meals.

Camping

Torness Camping Barn, at the southern end of the island, on the shore of Holland Bay near Leashun Loch, T01857-616314. Very basic and very cheap camping facilities. They also organize nature walks to the nearby seal-hide. Phone for pick-up from the ferry.

Westray p51

£££ Cleaton House Hotel, 2 miles southeast of Pierowall, T01857-677442, www.cleatonhouse.co.uk. 7 rooms. This converted Victorian manse is the best place to stay. Also serves excellent evening meals (3 courses **£££**).

£££ Pierowall Hotel, Pierowall, T01857-677472, www.pierowallhotel.co.uk. 4 en suite rooms. Less stylish than Cleaton House Hotel, but comfortable and friendly. Also serves good-value bar meals, try their fish and chips (**££**).

££ No 1 Broughton, Pierowall, T01857-677726, www.no1broughton.co.uk. Renovated house overlooking the bay, with 3 nicely furnished rooms. Packed lunch and light supper on request.

£ The Barn, Chalmersquoy, T01857-677214, www.thebarnwestray.co.uk. Sleeps 13 in 5 rooms. High-quality hostel accommodation with great views.

Bis Geos, T01857-677420, 677238, www. bisgeos.co.uk. 3 well-equipped self-catering cottages with great views. Minibus available from the pier. From £250 per week.

Papa Westray p52

££ School Place, T01857-644268. Homely B&B with lunch and evening meals available.

£ Beltane House Guest House, T01857-644321. A row of converted farm workers' cottages to the east of Holland House. It offers dinner (**££**). Run by the island community co-operative.

£ Papa Westray Hostel, T01857-644267, www.syha.org.uk. Open all year. In the same complex at **Beltane**. A 12-bed hostel run by the island community co-operative which also runs a shop and restaurant serving lunch and evening meals. They have a minibus which takes ferry passengers from the pier to anywhere on the island.

North Ronaldsay p53

££ Garso House, about 3 miles from the ferry pier, T01857-633244. Full-board B&B at Garso House. They also have a self-catering cottage – 'Brigg' – (sleeps up to 5 people) and can arrange car hire, taxis or minibus tours.

££ Observatory Guest House, T01857-633200, www.nrbo.co.uk. Offers wind- and solar-powered accommodation that's popular with birdwatchers and serves a great-value hearty dinner (**£**). It also has a small hostel next door (**£**).

❼ Restaurants

Eating options are very limited but most B&Bs and guesthouses will provide evening meals. See Where to stay on previous pages.

Kirkwall p36, map p37

£££-££ Lynnfield Hotel, Holm Rd, T01856-872505, www.lynnfieldhotel.com. Next to the Highland Park distillery, this hotel is renowned for its food, including bere bunno' (Orcadian bannocks) and cooked-to-perfection lobster and scallops.

££ Albert Hotel, Mounthoolie Lane, T01856-876000, www.alberthotel.co.uk. Serves decent bar meals made with home-grown produce. Variety of dining options available, from fine dining to traditional 'bothy' bar which is a favourite with locals and visitors.

Stromness and West Mainland p39

£££-££ Hamnavoe Restaurant, 35 Graham Pl, Stromness, T01856-850606. Apr-Oct Tue-Sun from 1900, Fri-Sat Nov-Mar 1200-1400, Sat-Sun from 1900. The best place to eat in town. It specializes in local seafood but also offers good vegetarian dishes.

££ Julia's Café and Bistro, opposite the ferry terminal, Stromness, T01856-850904. Mon-Sat 0900-1700, Sun 1000-1700. Open some evenings in summer. Very good home-cooked food and huge cakes right on the harbour.

££ Stromness Hotel, see Where to stay. Good bar meals and the hotel also has an à la carte restaurant. Children welcome.

£ Ferry Inn, near the ferry terminal, John St, Stromness, T01856-850280, www.ferryinn.com. Decent bar food and lively bar. Children welcome.

East Mainland and South Ronaldsay p43

£££ Creel Restaurant & Rooms, see also Where to stay. Superb food using deliciously fresh, locally grown ingredients. Dinner only. Best on the islands by some way.

£ Murray Arms Hotel, Back Rd, St Margaret's Hope, T01856-831205, www.murrayarms hotel.com. Not exactly haute cuisine but good-value bar meals served until 2100.

Hoy *p47*
££-£ Stromabank Hotel, Longhope, South Walls, T01856-701494, www.stromabank. co.uk. A bar and restaurant which serves local produce, including beef and lamb. Open to non-residents but book May-Sep.
£ Beneth'hill Café, 5 mins' walk from the Moaness ferry. Evening meals and early breakfasts served.

Rousay, Egilsay and Wyre *p48*
££-£ Pier Restaurant, Rousay, beside the pier, T01856-821359. Serves food at lunchtime (they stop serving at 1400) and evenings (last orders 1900) closed Wed and Sun. Standard or gourmet picnics can be ordered.

North Ronaldsay *p53*
££-£ Burrian Inn and Restaurant, T01857-633221. Orkney's most northerly pub, also serves food.

🎵 Bars and clubs

Kirkwall *p36, map p37*
Nightlife revolves around its lively pubs. Check in *The Orcadian* for folk nights, etc.
Ayre Hotel, see Where to stay. Quiet and relaxed but also stages folk music nights.
Bothy Bar, Albert Hotel, Mounthoolie Lane, T01856-876000, www.alberthotel.co.uk. A good place for a drink, and sometimes has live folk music.

Stromness and West Mainland *p39*
The best places for a drink in Stromness are the **Stromness Hotel**, see Where to stay; the **Ferry Inn**, 10 John St, T01865-850280; and the bar of the **Royal Hotel**, Victoria St, T01856-850342.

🎭 Entertainment

For details of what's going on, buy *The Orcadian*, www.orcadian.co.uk, which comes out on Thu, or pick up a free copy of the Tourist Board's guide.

Kirkwall *p36, map p37*
The town's **Phoenix cinema** is in the Pickaquoy Centre, Pickaquoy Rd, T01856-879900, www.pickaquoy.com. Also has sports and fitness facilities, a café and bar.

✺ Festivals

Orkney *p32*
There are numerous events which take place throughout the year.
May Orkney Folk Festival, www.orkney folkfestival.com. An excellent event, which takes place for 3 days at the end of May at various locations throughout the islands. It is always well attended and can be rather boisterous.
Jun St Magnus Festival, www.stmagnus festival.com. This high-brow event is one of the UK's most prestigious and popular festivals. Held in Kirkwall, it consists of six days of music, drama, literature and the visual arts, with many internationally renowned performers.
Jul Regattas, during this month there are several regattas held on most of the islands. Visit the TIC or read The Orcadian for more information.
Aug Festival of the Horse and Boys' Ploughing Match, South Ronaldsay, www.orkneyjar.com. There are numerous agricultural shows in Aug which culminate in this festival, see page 46.
Sep Orkney International Science Festival, T01343-540844, www.oisf.or. 1st week in Sep. Offers visitors the chance to participate in a range of talks and exhibitions about astronomy, zoology and even renewable energy. The week also includes a ceilidh and concerts.

To dive for

Orkney offers some of the best scuba-diving in the world, thanks to the part played by Scapa Flow in both world wars, see box, page 45. The wreckage on the sea bed, combined with the wildlife that teems around it – sea anemones, seals, whales and porpoises – make for great diving. Visibility is sharp and the water is not as cold as you expect, thanks to the Gulf Stream. Several companies offer diving courses for beginners and wreck diving for more experienced divers. This can be as a dive package, including accommodation, meals and boat charter, or simply as a boat charter. Most companies are based in Stromness, see below. For a list of dive operators, check out www.subaqua.co.uk.

Dec The Ba' (ball), in Kirkwall, www.ba gamecom. Amongst the best-known annual events. It takes place on Christmas Eve and New Year's Eve and is a bit like rugby, basketball and a full-scale riot all rolled into one, and is contested between 2 sides – the Uppies and the Doonies – representing different districts of the town. As many as 200 'players' may be involved, and a game can last up to 7 hrs as both sides attempt to jostle the ball along the streets until one reaches their 'goal' to win the prized ba'.

O Shopping

Kirkwall *p36, map p37*
The Odin Stone, 14 Junction Rd, T01856-877785, www.odinstone-orkney.co.uk. You can browse and buy the work of over 50 local crafts-folk at this delightful store.
Orkney Handcrafted Furniture, Dellovo, New Scapa Rd, T01856-872998. Authentic and award winning range of traditional Orkney chairs.
Ortak, Hatston, T01856-872224, www.ortak. co.uk Popular jewellery with designs that are influenced by Viking, runic carvings.

Stromness and West Mainland *p39*
Stromness Books and Prints, 1 Graham Pl, Stromness, T01856-850565. A wee gem. No '3 for 2' offers, no sofas, no internet, no skinny lattes with cinnamon, just books – ones that you might want to read – and an owner, Tam McPhail, who knows what he's talking about. A real bookshop for real people.

O What to do

Go-Orkney/Puffin Express, in Inverness, T01463-717181, www.go-orkney.com, run a full-day tour to Orkney from Inverness, visiting all the main sites. £485 for 2 people in high season, includes all transport.

Kirkwall *p36, map p37*
Tour operators
Orkney Ferries, Kirkwall, T01856-622260, www.orkneyferries.co.uk. Run the Eday Heritage Tour, book with Orkney Ferries or at the tourist office in Kirkwall.
Peedie Orkney Tours, 23 Willowburn Rd, T01856-879194, www.peedieorkneytours. com. Offer a wide variety of bespoke tours.

Stromness and West Mainland *p39*
Diving
The Diving Cellar, 4 Victoria St, Stromness, T01856-850055, www.divescapaflow.co.uk. Dive charter operating in Scapa Flow. Package including accommodation and minibus.
Scapa Flow Diving Holidays, Lerquoy, Outertown, Stromness, T01856-851110, www.scapa-flow.co.uk. Offers liveaboard packages or day trips on the *MV Invincible*.
Scapa Scuba, Lifeboat House, Stromness, T01856-851218, www.scapascuba.co.uk. Guided dives from £145 per person per day. Range of PADI courses available.

Tour operators
Wildabout Orkney, 5 Clouston Corner, Stenness, T01856-851011, www.wildabout orkney.com. Offers highly rated wildlife, historical, folklore and environmental tours. Their 'Treasures of Orkney' day tours costs £59 per person for a full day (child and concession reductions).

East Mainland and South Ronaldsway *p43*
Dawn Star Boat Trips, T01856-876743, www.orkneyboattrips.co.uk. Departing from the pier at St Mary's, Holm, these tours take you all round Scapa Flow with an emphasis on both history and wildlife. The boat holds 6 passengers so prices depend on how many are in your party (a 2-3 hr trip for 2 costs £100, for 6 it costs £160).
Orkney Aspects, Daisybank Farm, Deerness, T01856-741433, www.orkneyaspects.co.uk. Offers a variety of tours of the islands, including day tours which can be tailored to suit requirements.

Rousay, Egilsay and Wyre *p48*
Rousay Tours, T01856-821234. Run very informative minibus tours from Jun to early Sep Tue-Fri, meeting the 1040 ferry from Tingwall.

Shapinsay *p49*
Orkney Island Holidays, Furrowend, T01856-711373, www.ornkney.com. Paul and Louise Hollinrake have 20 years' experience running week-long all-inclusive tours of the island from their home base, with different holidays exploring the wildlife, archaeology, flora and fauna, history, crafts and local way of life on the islands.

Sanday *p50*
Roderick Thorne, Sanday Ranger, T01857-600341, ranger@sanday.co.uk. Guided walks and tours of the island.

Westray *p51*
Kenneth Harcus, Pierowall, T01857-677758. Runs a bus service round the island.

⊖ Transport

Check the **Loganair** website (www.loganair. co.uk) for all inter-island flights.

Kirkwall *p36, map p37*
Air Loganair, T01856-872494, flies Mon-Sat from Kirkwall to **Eday**, **Stronsay**, **Sanday** and **Westray** (£37 one way, £74 return) and to **North Ronaldsay** and **Papa Westray** (£18 one way, £36 return).

Bus There's a limited bus service around the Mainland, the timetables of which can be found at the TIC or on the transport pages of www.orkney.gov.uk. Stagecoach, T01856-870535, runs buses Mon-Sat from Kirkwall bus station to **Stromness**, 30 mins. It also runs 3-5 buses a day, Mon-Sat, to **Houton**, 35 mins, which connect with ferries to **Hoy**; and a daily bus, Mon-Sat, to **East Holm**, 25 mins, and **Stromness** via **Dounby**, 45 mins. There are buses daily to **St Margaret's Hope**, 30 mins and there are also buses to **Tingwall** and **Evie**. Note that there is a very restricted Sun bus service on Orkney.

Car hire Orkney Car Hire, Junction Rd, T01856-872666; WR Tullock, Castle St, T01856-876262, and Kirkwall airport, T01856-875500.

Cycle hire Cycle Orkney, Tankerness Lane, T01856-875777 www.cycleorkney.com. Mountain bikes from £10 per day.

Ferry Northlink Ferries, T0845-6000449, www.northlinkferries.co.uk, sails from Kirkwall to **Aberdeen**, Mon, Wed and Fri, 2345, 6 hrs. A single passenger fare costs £31 (peak season, Jul-Aug). A car costs £110. They also sail from Kirkwall to **Lerwick** (Shetland) on Tue, Thu, Sat and Sun, 2345, 7 hrs 45 mins. A passenger fare costs £24.30 single. A car costs £101 (in peak season).Return fares are double the cost of single fares and children under 16 travel for 50% less. Cars should be booked in advance and all passengers must check in at least 30 mins before departure. 2-berth cabins are available on all journeys, from £107 for a 4-berth inner cabin in peak season.

There are buses between Kirkwall and **Burwick**, 45 mins, to connect with all ferry sailings to John o'Groats (see below). John o'Groats Ferries also operate the Orkney Bus, a daily direct bus/ferry/bus service between Kirkwall and **Inverness**, via **John o'Groats**.

Stromness and West Mainland *p39*
Bus There are several buses Mon-Sat between Stromness and **Kirkwall**, 30 mins, via Hatston Ferry Terminal.

Car hire Brass's Car Hire, Blue Star Garage, North End Rd, Stromness, T01856-850850 www.stromnesscarhire.co.uk.

Cycle hire Orkney Cycle Hire, 54 Dundas St, Stromness, T01856-850255, www.orkneycyclehire.co.uk.

Ferry Northlink Ferries from Stromness to **Scrabster**, 1½ hrs. Passenger fare is £19.15 one-way in peak season and a car costs £58.

East Mainland and South Ronaldsay
p43
Ferry John o'Groats Ferries, T01955-611353, www.jogferry.co.uk, operates a passenger and bike-only ferry service from **Burwick** to **John o'Groats**.

Hoy *p47*
Ferry A passenger ferry sails between **Moaness Pier** and **Stromness**, daily, 30 mins. There's a reduced winter service (mid-Sep to mid-May).

Rousay, Egilsay and Wyre *p48*
Ferry A small car ferry operated by Orkney Ferries sails from **Rousay** to **Tingwall**, daily, 20 mins, with onward buses to **Kirkwall**.

Shapinsay *p49*
Ferry Small car ferry makes up to 6 sailings daily (including Sun in summer) to **Kirkwall** (25 mins).

Eday *p50*
Air There are flights from Eday to **Kirkwall** with **Loganair**, T01856-872494, Wed only.

Cycle hire Mr Burkett, at Hamarr, near the post office south of Mill Loch

Ferry Orkney Ferries sail to **Kirkwall** (1 hr 15 mins to 2 hrs) twice daily.

Taxi Mr A Stewart by the pier, T01857-622206.

Sanday *p50*
Air There are Loganair flights to **Kirkwall** twice daily Mon-Fri and once on Sat.

Ferry There's a ferry service twice daily to **Kirkwall**, 1½ hrs.

Stronsay *p51*
Air There are Loganair flights to **Kirkwall** twice daily Mon-Fri.

Car hire and taxis DS Peace, Samson's Lane, T01857-616335.

Ferry A ferry service runs to **Kirkwall** daily, 1½ hrs, and once daily Mon-Sat to **Eday**, 35 mins.

Westray *p51*
Air Loganair flights to **Kirkwall** depart twice daily Mon-Sat.

Cycle hire Alena, the proprietor of Bis Geos hostel on Westray, see Where to stay above, will hire out bikes for £5 per day. Barn Hostel, see Where to stay, is another high quality hostel that can arrange bike hire.

Ferry There's a car ferry service to **Kirkwall** from **Rapness**, 1½ hrs. It sails twice daily in summer (mid-May to mid-Sep) and once daily in winter. There's also a passenger ferry from **Pierowall** to **Papa Westray**.

Taxi Kenneth Harcus, T01857-677758.

Papa Westray *p52*

Air The 2-min flight to **Westray** leaves twice daily Mon-Sat, £17 one way. There is also a direct flight to **Kirkwall**, daily Mon-Sat, £18 one way.

Ferry There's a passenger ferry to **Pierowall** on Westray, 3-6 times daily, 25 mins.

North Ronaldsay *p53*

Air There are Loganair flights to **Kirkwall** twice daily Mon-Sat.

Ferry There's a car and passenger ferry which sails to **Kirkwall** twice a week (usually Tue and Fri), 2 hrs 40 mins.

⦿ Directory

Kirkwall *p36, map p37*
Banks Branches of the 3 main Scottish banks with ATMs are on Broad St and Albert St. Exchange also at the tourist office.
Laundry The Launderama, Albert St, T01856-872982. Mon-Fri 0830-1730, Sat 0900-1700. **Medical services** Balfour Hospital, Health Centre and Dental Clinic, New Scapa Rd, T01856-885400.
Post Junction Rd, Mon-Fri 0900-1700, Sat 0930-1230.

Stromness and West Mainland *p39*
Banks There are branches of Bank of Scotland and Royal Bank of Scotland, both with ATMs, on Victoria St, Stromness.
Laundry Next to the coffee shop, Stromness, T01856-850904, self-service or service washes.

Shetland

Shetland is so far removed from the rest of Scotland it can only be shown as an inset on maps. It is closer to the Arctic Circle than it is to London, and it's easier and quicker to get there from Norway than it is from the UK's capital. This seems entirely appropriate, for Shetland is historically and culturally closer to Scandinavia than Britain. Indeed, whilst the Scottish debate on independence waxes and wanes, so some Shetlanders argue that the Islands should go it alone. Many of its place names are of Norse origin, and people here still celebrate the Vikings in the annual Up-Helly-Aa festivals. Modern-day visitors tend to come by plane rather than longboat, and usually bring binoculars, for Shetland is a birdwatcher's paradise. It is home to countless species, many of them seeking refuge from the madding crowds. And there's no better place than here to get away from it all. Moreover, due to its latitude, in high summer there's daylight for more than 20 hours of day so if you want to pack as much as possible into your visit this is the place where you can enjoy a coastal walk or round of golf at midnight.

Arriving in Shetland

Getting there

Air Getting to Shetland by air can be expensive. Though there are seats available online from around £39, expect to pay from £100 one way from Aberdeen and over £200 return. Shetland has good air connections with the rest of the UK and there are regular flights from several mainland airports which are operated by **Flybe** ① *T0871-700 2000, www.flybe.com* or **Loganair** ① *T01595-840246, www.loganair.co.uk*. There are direct daily flights from Aberdeen, which has frequent services to all other major British airports and there are also direct flights from Glasgow (daily), Edinburgh (Monday to Saturday), Inverness (Monday to Friday), Orkney (Monday to Saturday) and Belfast (Sunday to Friday). There are also regular international flights from Bergen (Norway).

Shetland's main **airport** ① *T01950-460654*, is at Sumburgh, 25 miles south of Lerwick and there are regular daily buses (No 6), which connect with flights. These buses also stop at several main sights, including Jarlshof and Sandwick (for Mousa Broch).

Sea Ferry links with the UK are provided mostly by **Northlink Ferries** ① *T0845-600 0449, www.northlinkferries.co.uk*. It operates daily car ferry sailings to Lerwick from Aberdeen

Shetland

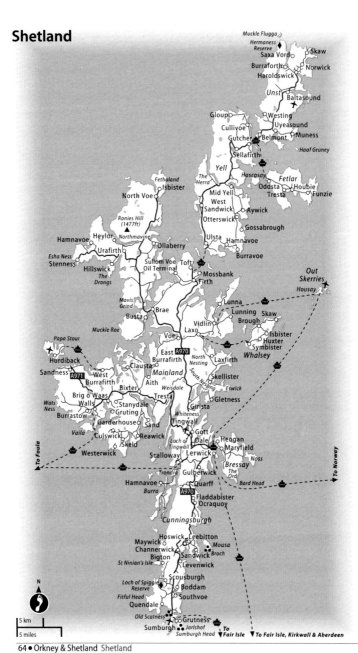

(some are via Kirkwall, Orkney), the journey takes 12 hours (14 hours if it goes via Kirkwall). There are also ferries from Norway, Iceland and the Faroe Isles. ▸▸ *For further information, see Transport, page 82.*

Getting around

There is a regular scheduled inter-island service with **Directflight** ① *T01595-840246, www.directflight.co.uk*, from Tingwall airport near Lerwick to Foula, Fair Isle, Papa Stour and Out Skerries. An extensive public bus service links Lerwick with all towns, villages and tourist sights (there are several operators). Bus No 4 runs to Scalloway (Monday to Saturday) and there are also buses (Monday to Saturday) to Walls (No 9), Sandness, Aith (No 9 and 12), North Roe (No 21), Hillswick (No 21), Vidlin (No19), Toft (No 23) and Mossbank (No 23). Buses leave from the **Viking bus station** ① *Commercial Rd, T01595-694100, Mon-Sat 0900-1715,* in Lerwick to destinations all over the Mainland.

Frequent ferry services also link many of the islands with the Shetland mainland. These services are operated by **Shetland Islands Council** ① *T01595-693535, www.shetland. gov.uk.* Fares vary according the route and booking in advance is essential. Times and fares can be found on the Shetland Council website or are available from the TIC in Lerwick. A *Shetland Transport Timetable*, published by the Shetland Council, contains details of all air, sea and bus services throughout the islands. It is available from the tourist office in Lerwick. Note that fares quoted in the transport section are for return trips. Shetland has around 500 miles of good roads, and the best way to explore the islands is by car, but note that it is cheaper to hire a car in Lerwick rather than at the airport. Hitching is a feasible way to get around and is relatively safe, and cycling is a good way to experience the islands, though most places are very exposed and the winds can be relentless and punishing (Force 8 is considered pleasant in these parts). ▸▸ *For further details, see Transport page 82.*

Tourist information

The main tourist office is the **Lerwick TIC** ① *Market Cross, Commercial St, T08701-999440, May-Sep Mon-Fri 0800-1800, Sat 0800-1600, Sun 1000-1300, Oct-Apr Mon-Fri 0900-1700,* which is an excellent source of information, books, maps and leaflets. They will also change foreign currency and book accommodation. It's also worth checking out the excellent www.visitshetland.com, with links to events, transport, accommodation and local operators.

Lerwick and around → *For listings, see pages 76-84. Phone code 01595. Population 7600.*

Lerwick is the capital and administrative centre of Shetland and the only sizeable town, containing over 7000 of the islands' 22,000 strong population. Though the islands have been inhabited for many centuries, Lerwick only dates from the 17th century, when it began to grow as a trading port for Dutch herring fishermen, thanks to its superb natural sheltered harbour, the Bressay Sound. The town spread along the waterfront, where merchants built their lodberries, which were houses and warehouses with their own piers so that they could trade directly with visiting ships. By the late 19th century Lerwick had become the main herring port in northern Europe. Lerwick has continued to grow: the discovery of oil in the North Sea in the early 1970s led to the building of the Sullom Voe Oil Terminal, and the effect on the town has been dramatic. It is now the main transit point to the North Sea oil rigs and there have been major extensions to the harbour area, bringing increased shipping and prosperity to the town.

Arriving in Lerwick

Getting there and around Ferries from Aberdeen arrive at the main Holmsgarth terminal, about a mile north of the old harbour. There's a regular bus service between Lerwick and Sumburgh airport (50 minutes) run by **John Leask & Son** ① *T01595-693162, www.leaskstravel.co.uk.* Taxis (around £25) and car hire are also available. All island bus services start and end at the Viking bus station, which is on Commercial Road, a short distance north of the town centre. The town, with about six pubs – including the Thule bar, frequented by hardy fishermen – is small and everything is within easy walking distance.

Places in Lerwick

The town's heart is the attractive **Commercial Street**, which runs parallel to the Esplanade. At the southern end are many old houses and lodberries, and you can continue south along the cliffs to the **Knab** or to lovely **Bain's beach**. Lerwick Walks is a leaflet detailing many interesting walks in and around town.

Lerwick

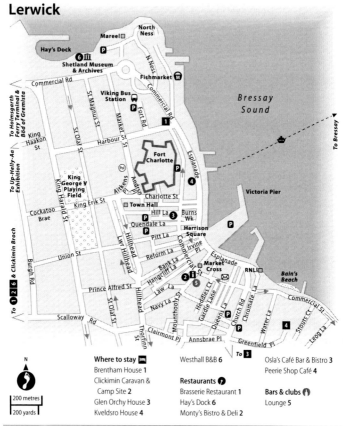

Where to stay 🛏
Brentham House **1**
Clickimin Caravan &
  Camp Site **2**
Glen Orchy House **3**
Kveldsro House **4**

Westhall B&B **6**

Restaurants 🍴
Brasserie Restaurant **1**
Hay's Dock **6**
Monty's Bistro & Deli **2**

Osla's Café Bar & Bistro **3**
Peerie Shop Café **4**

Bars & clubs 🍸
Lounge **5**

200 metres
200 yards

Overlooking the north end of Commercial Street is **Fort Charlotte** ① *Jun-Sep daily 0900-2200, Oct-May daily 0900-1600, free,* built in 1665 and later rebuilt in 1780 and named after Queen Charlotte, George III's consort. It has since been used as a prison and Royal Naval Reserve base and, though there's little to see in the fort, there are fine views of the harbour from the battlements. (As an aside, if you're hungry, the Fort chip shop below the fort by the war memorial serves up cheap and tasty fish suppers.) One of Lerwick's most impressive buildings is the Victorian **town hall** ① *Mon-Fri 1000-1200, 1400-1530, free,* on Hillhead. The stained-glass windows of the main hall depict episodes from Shetland's history. Built on the historic site of Hay's Dock, is the fabulous **Shetland Museum and Archives** ① *T01595-695057, www.shetland-museum.org.uk, Mon-Sat 1000-1700, Sun 1200-1700, free,* which uses interactive technology to give an introduction to the islands' history. Amongst the artefacts on display are Viking runes, whale bones carved by fishermen and all manner of things knitted in the Fair Isle style. Next to the museum, housed in an impressive new building, is **Mareel** ① *www.mareel.org, Sun-Thu 1000-2300, Fri-Sat 1000-0100,* a live music, cinema and creative arts centre managed by Shetland Arts Development Agency. The café is a great place for a quick lunch or a drink and a snack in the evening.

Also in town, in the Galley Shed off St Sunniva Street, is the **Up-Helly-Aa Exhibition** ① *www.uphellyaa.org, mid-May to mid-Sep Tue 1400-1600, 1700-1900, Fri 1700-1900, Sat 1400-1600, £3, concessions and children £1.* This gives a taste of the famous fire festivals, the biggest of which is held annually in Lerwick on the last Tuesday in January, when there's a torch-lit procession through the town with hundreds of people dressed in Viking costumes (*guizers*). The procession is followed by a replica Viking longship built especially for the event. At the end of the procession the ship is set ablaze when the guizers throw their flaming torches on to it.

A mile west of town are the substantial remains of **Clickimin Broch**, a fortified site occupied from 700 BC to around the fifth or sixth century AD. A path leads to the site from opposite the supermarket on the A970. About a mile north of the ferry terminal is the **Böd of Gremista Museum** ① *T01595-695057, May to mid-Sep Tue-Sat 1000-1300, 1400-1700, free,* a restored 18th-century fishing *böd* (booth) which was the birthplace of Arthur Anderson (1791-1868), co-founder of the Peninsular and Oriental Steam Navigation Company, now P&O. One of the rooms features an exhibition on Anderson's life and involvement with P&O.

Bressay

Lying to the east of Lerwick across the Bressay Sound is the island of Bressay (pronounced 'bressah'), which creates a sheltered harbour for the capital and led to its establishment as a major trading port. Seven miles long by three miles wide, it makes an ideal day trip for cyclists. Another good way to get around is on foot, and there's a fine walk to the top of **Ward Hill** (742 ft), the highest point, from where you get great views of the island and as far afield as Foula and Out Skerries. There are also good coastal walks, particularly along the cliffs from Noss Sound south to **Bard Head**, **The Ord** and **Bressay Lighthouse**, where you can see large colonies of seabirds. For wildlife cruises to Bressay and Noss, see page 82.

Noss

Serious birdwatchers should head for Noss, a tiny, uninhabited island off the east coast of Bressay, which is a **National Nature Reserve** with over 100,000 pairs of breeding seabirds. A walk around the perimeter of the island takes at least three hours but is highly recommended. At the east side is the **Noup of Noss**, where the 600-ft cliffs are packed full of nesting gannets. The reserve is managed by Scottish Natural Heritage who have a small visitor centre at **Gungstie**.

Central Mainland → *For listings, see pages 76-84. See map, page 64. Phone code 01595.*

The Central Mainland is Shetland's slim waist, where only a few miles of land separate the east and west coast. There's not a huge amount of tourist interest here but the area's history is fascinating and the Scalloway Museum is certainly worth a visit.

Scalloway and around

Six miles from Lerwick on the west coast is Scalloway, once the capital of Shetland and now a fishing port and fish-processing centre. In 1942, during the Second World War, Scalloway became the headquarters of the **Shetland Bus** operations. This was the name given to the Norwegian fishing boats which sailed to Shetland during the night from German-occupied Norway, bringing refugees to safety and returning with ammunition and resistance fighters. An interesting and poignant exhibition on the Shetland Bus can be seen at **Scalloway Museum** ① *Main St, T01595-880608, May-Sep Mon-Sat 1000-1200, 1400-1630, free.*

The harbour is dominated by the ruins of **Scalloway Castle** (the key is available from the Shetland Woollen Company or on a Sunday, the Scalloway Hotel), built in 1600 by the notorious Earl Patrick Stewart using local slave labour (see box, page 38). After his execution the castle fell into disrepair, though the four-storey main block and one wing remain. Inside, an interpretative display explains its history.

South of Scalloway lie the islands of **Trondra** and **Burra**, now connected to the Mainland by bridges. At the south of the promontory at Houss, East Burra is the workshop of **Burra Bears** (call to arrange a visit T01595-859374, www.burrabears.co.uk), where you can buy teddy bears made from recycled Fair Isle jumpers. On the road back, over towards West Burra is the attractive little fishing village of **Hamnavoe**.

Tingwall

North of Scalloway, the B9074 runs through the fertile Tingwall Valley, past a nine-hole **golf course** at Asta and the **Loch of Tingwall**, which is good for brown trout fishing and also home to swans and otters. At the northern end of the loch is a promontory called **Law Ting Holm**, which was the site of the Althing, or parliament, during the period of Norse rule. Overlooking the loch is **Tingwall Kirk**, built in the late 18th century on the site of the earlier church of St Magnus which dated back to the early period of Norse Christianity. In the graveyard is the old burial vault with several interesting old grave slabs. Nearby is **Tingwall Agricultural Museum** ① *T01595-840770, Jun-Aug Mon-Sat 1000-1300, 1400-1700, £2,* which houses a collection of old crofting implements.

Weisdale

The A971 continues northwest towards Weisdale, a district with some worthwhile attractions. At the head of **Weisdale Voe** the B9075 branches north to **Weisdale Mill** ① *T01595-830400, Tue-Sat 1030-1630, Sun 1200-1630, free (also café Tue-Sat 1100-1600, Sun 1200-1600),* which houses the **Bonhoga Gallery**, a purpose-built art gallery featuring varied exhibitions of local, national and international works. There's also a nice café serving snacks. Weisdale Mill was part of the Kergord Estate, known until 1945 as Flemington, and was built from the stones of evacuated crofthouses. Over 300 crofters were forcibly evicted in the mid-19th century during the Clearances, when lairds expanded their more profitable sheep-farming activities. In 1940 the mill was requisitioned as the intelligence and administrative HQ for the **Shetland Bus** operations (see Scalloway, above). The Kergord estate today is the largest area of woodland in Shetland and attracts migratory birds.

On the west shore of Weisdale Voe, south of the mill, are the ruins of the house where John Clunies Ross (1786-1854) was born. He settled in the Cocos Islands in the Indian Ocean in 1827; the islands were owned by the Estate of the Clunies Ross family until purchased by the Australian government in 1978. In 1984 the islanders voted to become part of Australia.

The Westside → *For listings, see pages 76-84. Phone code 01595. OS Landranger Nos 3 & 4.*

The western Mainland of Shetland, stretching west from Weisdale to Sandness, is known as The Westside. This part of Shetland is notable for its varied landscape of spectacular sea cliffs, rolling green hills, bleak moorland, peaty freshwater lochs and numerous long sea lochs, or voes. This is excellent walking country, with many fine coastal routes, especially around **Culswick** and **Dale of Walls**. It is also great for birdwatching and trout fishing, and there are many opportunities for spotting whales, dolphins and otters.

Stanydale, Walls and Sandness

There are a few interesting archaeological sites here, too. At Stanydale, signposted from the road between the villages of **Bixter** and **Walls**, is the site of a Neolithic settlement with the remains of houses, field boundaries and clearance cairns. Near the **Brig o' Waas**, just north of Walls, is the **Scord of Brouster**, a prehistoric farm which has been excavated.

The pretty little village of **Walls** (pronounced *waas*) is set around a sheltered natural harbour and is a popular spot with visiting yachts. It also attracts many visitors during its Agricultural Show in August, the biggest such event on Shetland. Walls is the departure point for ferries to the remote island of Foula, see below.

Northwest of Walls, the A971 crosses bleak moorland before descending to the crofting township of **Sandness** (pronounced *saa-ness*), surrounded by fertile land and facing little Papa Stour, about a mile offshore. There's a good beach here and also a **woollen spinning mill** where you can watch how they spin the famously fine wool into yarn.

Foula

Lying 15 miles west of the Shetland Mainland, tiny Foula – whose name derives from the Norse *fugl ey*, meaning 'bird island' – is the second most remote inhabited island after Fair Isle. It supports a population of around 40 people, who are greatly outnumbered by the many thousands of seabirds, including a small colony of gannets and the rare Leach's petrel. There are also about 2500 pairs of great skuas, the largest colony in the UK. The island is dominated by its sheer cliffs, which reach their peak at **The Kame** (1220 ft), the second-highest sea cliffs in Britain after St Kilda.

An interesting feature of the island's people is that they still observe the old Julian calendar replaced in 1752 in Britain by the present Gregorian system which deleted 11 days from the year. Remote areas of the country kept to the old calendar, adding an extra day in 1800, which was a leap year, and some parts of Shetland continued to observe festivals 12 days after the dates in the new calendar. The most remote areas kept to the old calendar longest, and the people of Foula still celebrate Christmas on 6 January and New Year's Day on 13 January.

Papa Stour

A ferry sails from West Burrafirth on the Westside, near Sandness, to the little island of Papa Stour, only a mile offshore. The island, which has a population of around 30, is mostly made up of volcanic rock which has been eroded to form an amazing coastline of stacks, arches and caves, most spectacular of which is **Kirstan's Hole**. The island is home to large colonies of auks, terns and skuas, and also has an interesting history of its own. Pick up the island trails leaflet from the tourist office in Lerwick.

South Mainland → *For listings, see pages 76-84. Phone code 01950.*

From Lerwick a long, narrow finger of land points south. The main road runs down the east coast for 25 miles till it ends at **Sumburgh Head**, near Shetland's main airport. This southern part of the Shetland Mainland holds the islands' two most important archaeological sights and main tourist attractions.

Isle of Mousa

ⓘ *For details of trips to the island, see What to do, page 82.*

Some 15 miles south of Lerwick, the scattered crofting communities of Sandwick look across to the Isle of Mousa, site of the best-preserved broch in Scotland. This fortified tower was built around 2000 years ago and still stands close to its original height of 45 ft. It's a very impressive structure when you see it from the inside and has chambers, galleries, an internal staircase and a parapet. The broch features in a Viking saga of the 12th century when the mother of Harald, Earl of Orkney, took refuge there with her lover. The Earl, who did not approve of the liaison, laid siege to the broch, but it proved impregnable and he gave up.

Mousa island is also home to many seabirds and waders, most notably the storm petrel – or alamootie, as the locals call it – which is best seen at dusk as it returns to its nest amongst the beach rocks. **Mousa Boat Trips** run late evening trips from late May to mid-July to see storm petrels swarm the broch: a sight, sound and indeed a vibration you will never forget. You can also see seals on the white sand beach at West Voe. If you have time, it's a good idea to walk right around the coast, starting from the landing stage at West Ham and first heading south to the broch. Watch out for dive-bombing bonxies (arctic terns).

South of Sandwick

Further south on the east coast, at Boddam, is the **Shetland Crofthouse Museum**
ⓘ *T01595-695057, May-Sep daily 1000-1300, 1400-1700, donations welcome*, a restored thatched crofthouse built in the early 19th century. This was inhabited by a crofting family until the 1960s, with the women working the land whilst the men went fishing or whaling. The two rooms – the but and the ben – hold all the original furnishings and utensils and there is a typical kale yard and upturned boat shed outside. During the evenings of the summer months, Elma Johnson of **Island Trails** (see Tours) tells old Shetland stories by the fireside. For more information check with the TIC in Lerwick.

St Ninian's Isle to Quendale

On the west coast, near Bigton village, a signposted track leads to the spectacular sandy causeway (known as an ayre or tombolo) which leads to St Ninian's Isle. The tombolo is the best example of its kind in Britain, and you can walk across to the island which is best

Close encounters of the bird kind

Shetland is famous for its birds. As well its huge seabird colonies, the islands attract Arctic species and are an important crossroads for migrating birds. Over 340 species have been recorded on Fair Isle, including rare and exotic birds from Asia and America. Twenty-one out of the 24 seabirds common to Britain breed in Shetland. These can be found around the coastline, but the largest colonies are at the Hermaness and Noss reserves.

Amongst the many species which can be seen are the puffin. About one fifth of Scotland's puffins breed in Shetland. Its cousins in the auk family, guillemots, and razorbills, are also here in abundance during the summer months, along with kittiwakes, shags and that most common of seabirds, the fulmar. Britain's largest seabird, the gannet, can be seen diving spectacularly for fish at Hermaness, Noss, Fair Isle and Foula, while its smallest seabird, the storm petrel, is best seen around dusk on the tiny island of Mousa.

Summer heralds the return of the Arctic tern which breeds along low coastlines, as do the eider, oystercatcher, ringed plover and black guillemot, or tystie, which stays here all year round. The best place to see waders and

shelduck are the nutrient-rich tidal mudflats at the Pool of Virkie in the South Mainland.

Many birds breed on agricultural land, and these include the lapwing, skylark, meadow pipit and wheater. The hills and moorland provide breeding grounds for many summer visitors such as that pirate of the skies, the great skua, or bonxie, and the Arctic skua. Another Arctic species, the whimbrel, also nests here, mainly in Unst, Yell and Fetlar. Moorland habitats are also favoured by the curlew, golden plover and merlin, Shetland's only bird of prey, while the lochs are home to large numbers of red-throated divers. Fetlar is home to 90% of the population of one of Britain's rarest birds, the red-necked phalarope.

Many of Shetland's bird habitats are protected as RSPB Reserves and National Nature Reserves, and it is an offence to disturb the birds and their young at or near their nests. You also risk being dive-bombed by some of the more aggressively protective species. For a full list of all species recorded on the islands and more practical bird-watching information, get a copy of the *Shetland Bird Chart*, by Joyce Gammack, available from the tourist office in Lerwick.

known for the hoard of Pictish treasure which was discovered in 1958 in the ruins of the 12th-century church. The 28 silver objects included bowls, a spoon and brooches, probably dating from around AD 800, and are now on display in the Royal Scottish Museum in Edinburgh, though you can see replicas in the Shetland Museum in Lerwick.

The west coast south of Bigton is beautiful with long, sandy beaches interspersed with dramatic cliff scenery. On the other side of the road from the long, sheltered beach at **Scousburgh Sands** is the **Loch of Spiggie RSPB Reserve**. The loch is an important winter wildfowl refuge, particularly for wooper swans, and during the summer you can see various ducks, waders, gulls, terns and skuas. There's a hide on the northern shore with an information board. Nearby is the **Spiggie Hotel** which offers afternoon tea or dinner.

A few miles south of the loch is the village of **Quendale**, overlooking a wide, sandy bay. Here you'll find the beautifully restored and fully working 19th-century **Quendale Mill** ① *T01950-460969, www.quendalemill.shetland.co.uk, Apr-Oct daily 1000-1700, £2, craft shop and tourist information point*, the last of Shetland's watermills. You might not see it, but you will hear the groan of the wreck of the Braer oil tanker that lies between Garth's

Ness and Fitful Head. It ran on to the rocks in 1993. A disaster of epic proportions was averted by the hurricane-force gales which dispersed the huge oil spillage.

Sumburgh and Jarlshof

At the southern tip of Mainland is the village of Sumburgh, site of Shetland's main airport for external passenger flights and for helicopters and planes servicing the North Sea oil industry. South of the airport is Shetland's prime archaeological site, **Jarlshof** ① *T01950-460112, late Mar-Sep daily 0930-1730, £5.50, concessions £4.40, children £3.30*, a hugely impressive place which spans 4000 years of occupation from Neolithic times through Norse settlement to the 16th century. The original Stone Age dwellings are topped by a broch, Pictish wheelhouses, Viking longhouses and, towering over the whole complex, the ruins of a 16th-century mansion. This remarkable site was only discovered at the end of the 19th century when a violent storm ripped off the top layer of turf. Jarlshof is, in fact, not a genuine name, but the exotic invention of Sir Walter Scott in his novel *The Pirate*. A useful guidebook available from the visitor centre helps bring the place to life.

Another fascinating excavation has been going on nearby, at **Old Scatness** ① *T01595-694688, www.shetlandamenity.org, visitors are welcome at the site on Sun in Jul only, 1000-1700, adults £5, concessions £4, group visits at other times by arrangement (£100 for up to 25 people)*, and looks set to become just as impressive. Since 1995, a team from Bradford University have been working here and have revealed a mound over 5 m high and 80 m in diameter thought to have been inhabited for over 3000 years. In its centre is an Iron Age tower, or broch.

South of Jarlshof, the Mainland ends abruptly at **Sumburgh Head**, an RSPB Reserve. The **lighthouse** on top of the cliff was built by Robert Stevenson in 1821, and the keepers' cottages are now rented out as self-catering accommodation. The lighthouse isn't open to the public, but from its grounds you can see many nesting seabirds such as puffins, kittiwakes, fulmars, guillemots and razorbills. To the east of the airport is **Pool of Virkie**, a good birdwatching area.

Fair Isle → *For listings, see pages 76-84. Phone code 01595.*

Fair Isle, 24 miles southwest of Sumburgh and 27 miles northeast of North Ronaldsay in Orkney, is the most isolated of Britain's inhabited islands. Only three miles long by 1½ miles wide, the island has a population of around 70 and is best known for its intricately patterned knitwear, which is still produced by a co-operative, **Fair Isle Crafts**. Co-operative could be said to sum up the friendly islanders, whose lifestyle is based on mutual help and community effort.

Arriving in Fair Isle

Getting to Fair Isle requires patience, persistence and a strong stomach to survive the white-knuckle 4½-hour ferry journey, booked through **Good Shepherd** ① *T01595-760363, £5 each way*. There are also flights from Tingwall airport, Monday to Saturday. A return flight costs £76 (£51 for ages 12-24, £38 for ages 2-11). You can also fly from Kirkwall on Orkney, which allows 2½ hours on the island, T01856-872420. For more information on Fair Isle and on boat and flight times visit www.fairisle.org.uk, or call the **National Trust for Scotland** ① *T0844-493-2100, www.nts.org.uk*. ▸▸ *For further details, see Transport page 83.*

Places in Fair Isle

Fair Isle is a paradise for birdwatchers, and keen ornithologists form the majority of the island's visitors. Celebrity birdwatcher and former Goodie, Bill Oddie, has dubbed it the 'the Hilton of the bird world'. It stands in the flight path of many thousands of migrating birds, and over 340 species have been recorded here at the **Fair Isle Bird Observatory** ① *T01595-760258, www.fairislebirdobs.co.uk, Apr-Oct*, which also offers accommodation and where visitors are welcome to take part. As well as the almost obscenely rich birdlife, there are around 240 species of flowering plants, making the island an especially beautiful haven for naturalists. Fair Isle's coastline, especially in the north and west, also boasts some outstanding cliff scenery.

The bird observatory was the brainchild of George Waterston, an ornithologist who first visited in 1935 and then bought the island in 1948 to begin his task of building the observatory. The island was given to the National Trust for Scotland in 1954 and declared a National Scenic Area. It was also designated a place of outstanding natural beauty and cultural heritage by the Council of Europe. The **George Waterston Memorial Centre** ① *T01595-760244, May to mid-Sep Mon and Fri 1400-1600, Wed 1000-1200, donations welcome*, has exhibits and photographs detailing the island's natural history, as well as the history of crofting, fishing, archaeology and knitwear. **The Textile Workshop** ① *T01595-760248, open year round by prior arrangement,,* offers demonstrations in textile techniques. Individuals and small groups can be accommodated for short courses.

North Mainland → *For listings, see pages 76-84. Phone code 01806.*

The main road north from Lerwick branches at **Voe**, a peaceful and colourful little village nestling in a bay at the head of the Olna Firth. One branch leads to the Yell car and passenger ferry terminal at **Toft**, past the turn-off to the massive **Sullom Voe Oil Terminal**, the largest oil and liquefied gas terminal in Europe. The other road heads northwest to Brae (see below).

Brae and Muckle Roe

Brae is not a very pretty place and was built to accommodate workers at the nearby Sullom Voe oil terminal. However, it does boast a good selection of accommodation and decent facilities – such as Frankie's, Britain's most northerly fish and chip shop – and makes a good base from which to explore the wild and wonderful coastal scenery around the Northmavine peninsula to the north. There's also good walking and spectacularly good westerly views around the island of **Muckle Roe** to the southwest, and up the island's small hill, **South Ward** (554 ft). But be careful of the overly protective bonxies, which will attack if you get too close to their nests in the grass. The island is attached to the mainland by a bridge.

Northmavine

The charmingly named **Mavis Grind**, the narrow isthmus where it's claimed you can throw a stone from the Atlantic to the North Sea, leads into Northmavine, the northwest peninsula of North Mainland. It is one of Shetland's most dramatic and beautiful areas, with rugged scenery, spectacular coastline and wide empty spaces. This is wonderful walking country, and it's a good idea to abandon the car and explore it on foot. **Hillswick Ness**, to the south of **Hillswick** village, is a nice walk, but further west, around the coastline of **Eshaness**, is the most spectacular cliff scenery and amazing natural features, all with unusual and evocative names.

North of the lighthouse are the **Holes of Scraada**, **Grind o' da Navir** and the **Villians of Hamnavoe**, which are not the local gangs but eroded lava cliffs with blowholes, arches and caves. East of Eshaness are the **Heads of Grocken** and **The Drongs**, a series of exposed sea stacks, which offer superb diving. Further north, overlooking the deep sea inlet of **Ronies Voe**, is the dramatic red-granite bulk of **Ronies Hill** (1477 ft), with a well-preserved burial cairn at the summit. The coastal scenery to the north and west of here is even more breathtaking, but very remote and exposed. You should be well equipped before setting out.

Between Eshaness and Hillswick, a side road leads south to the **Tangwick Haa Museum** ① *T01806-503347, Apr-Sep daily 1100-1700, free*, which features displays and photographs on the history of fishing and whaling and the hardships of life in these parts.

Whalsay and Out Skerries → *For listings, see pages 76-84. Phone code 01806.*

South of Voe, the B9071 branches east to **Laxo**, the ferry terminal for the island of **Whalsay**. There are regular daily car ferries for £3.60 per passenger and £8.50 per car including driver. The journey takes 30 minutes. Whalsay is one of Shetland's most prosperous small islands owing to its thriving paelagic fishing industry, which helps support a population of around 1000. There are rumoured to be more millionaires here per head of population that anywhere else in Scotland. Certainly its golf course above the cliffs is rich with sea views. In the seas around Whalsay you can see porpoises, dolphins, minke whales and orcas, hence its viking name which means 'island of whales'. The fishing fleet is based at **Symbister**, the island's main settlement. Beside the harbour at Symbister is the **Pier House**, a restored böd (see box page 79) which was used by the Hanseatic League, a commercial association of German merchants who traded in Shetland from the Middle Ages to the early 18th century. Inside is an exhibition explaining the history of the Hanseatic trade, and general information on the island. One of Scotland's great poets, Hugh McDiarmid (Christopher Grieve), spent most of the 1930s in Whalsay, where he wrote much of his finest poetry, until he was called for war work in 1942, never to return. His former home, at Sodom near Symbister, is now a camping böd, see Where to stay, page 78.

The Out Skerries is a small group of rocky islands about five miles from Whalsay and 10 miles east of Shetland Mainland. It's made up of three main islands: the larger islands of **Housay** and **Bruray**, which are connected by a road bridge; and the uninhabited island of **Grunay**. The Skerries boast some spectacular and rugged sea cliffs which are home to many rare migrant seabirds in spring and autumn.

Yell, Fetlar and Unst → *For listings, see pages 76-84.*

Yell → *Phone code 01957.*
Yell, the second largest of the Shetland Islands, was described rather damningly by the Orkney-favouring writer Eric Linklater, as 'dull and dark'. And it's true that the interior is consistently desolate peat moorland. But the coastline is greener and more pleasant and provides an ideal habitat for the island's large otter population. Yell is also home to a rich variety of birds, and offers some good coastal and hill walks, especially around the rugged coastline of **The Herra**, a peninsula about halfway up the west coast.

At **Burravoe**, about five miles east of the ferry terminal at **Ulsta**, is the **Old Haa Museum** ① *T01957-722339, late Apr-Sep Tue-Thu and Sat 1000-1600, Sun 1400-1700, free, donations* *appreciated, garden open every day*, housed in Yell's oldest building which dates from 1672. It contains an interesting display on local flora and fauna and history.

The island's largest village, **Mid Yell**, has a couple of shops, a pub and a leisure centre with a good swimming pool. About a mile northwest, on the hillside above the main road, are the reputedly haunted ruins of **Windhouse**, dating from 1707. To the north is the **RSPB Lumbister Reserve**, where red-throated divers, merlins, great and Arctic skuas and many other bird species come to breed. The reserve is also home to a large population of otters. A pleasant walk leads along the nearby steep and narrow gorge, known as the **Daal of Lumbister**, filled with many colourful flowers. The area to the north of the reserve provides good walking over remote moorland and coastline.

The road continues north past the reserve and around **Basta Voe**, where you can see otters. North of **Gutcher**, the ferry port for Unst, is the village of **Cullivoe**, with some good walks along the attractive coastline. There's a bus service which runs between Ulsta and Cullivoe and stops at villages in between, T01975-744214.

Fetlar → *Phone code 01957.*
Fetlar is the smallest of the North Isles but the most fertile and is known as 'the garden of Shetland'. Indeed, the name derives from Norse meaning 'fat land', as there is good grazing and croftland and a wide variety of plant and bird life. The whole island is good for birdwatching, but the prime place is the 1700 acres of **North Fetlar RSPB Reserve** around Vord Hill (522 ft) in the north of the island. This area has restricted access during the summer months, and visitors should contact the warden at Bealance (T01957-733246). The warden will also let you know if and when you can see the one or two female snowy owls which sometime visit.

The north cliffs of the reserve are home to large colonies of breeding seabirds, including auks, gulls and shags, and you can also see common and grey seals on the beaches in late autumn. Fetlar is home to one of Britain's rarest birds, the red-necked phalarope, which breeds in the loch near **Funzie** (pronounced 'finnie') in the east of the island. You can watch them from the RSPB hide in the nearby marshes. Red-throated divers and whimbrel also breed here. The island is also good for walking, and a leaflet describing some of the walks is available from the tourist office in Lerwick.

The main settlement on the island is **Houbie** on the south coast. Here you'll see a house called Leagarth, which was built by the island's most famous son, Sir William Watson Cheyne, who, with Lord Lister, pioneered antiseptic surgery. Nearby is the excellent **Fetlar Interpretive Centre** ① *T01957-733206, www.fetlar.com, May-Sep Mon-Fri 1100-1500, Sat-Sun 1300-1600, £2, concessions £1, under 16s free*, which presents the island's history and gives information on its bounteous birdlife.

Unst → *Phone code 01957.*
Unst is the most northerly inhabited island in Britain and some believe it is where the Vikings first landed on Shetland, but there is more to the island than its many 'most northerly' credentials. Aside from being where the local bakery makes 'oceanic' oatcakes from sea water, it is scenically one of the most varied of the Shetland Islands, with spectacular cliffs, sea stacks, sheltered inlets, sandy beaches, heather-clad hills, fertile farmland, freshwater lochs and even a sub-arctic desert. Such a variety of habitats supports over 400 plant species and a rich variety of wildlife. Unst is a major breeding site for gannets, puffins, guillemots, razorbills, kittiwakes, shags, Arctic and great skuas and whimbrels, amongst others, and in the surrounding waters you can see seals, porpoises, otters and even killer whales.

In the east of the island, north of **Baltasound**, is the **Keen of Hamar National Nature Reserve**, 74 acres of serpentine rock which breaks into tiny fragments known as 'debris', giving the landscape a strange, lunar-like appearance. This bleak 'desert' is actually home to some of the rarest plants in Britain. Baltasound is the island's main settlement, with an airport, hotel, pub, post office, leisure centre with pool and Britain's most northerly brewery, the **Valhalla Brewery** ① *T01975-711658, www.valhallabrewery.co.uk, visited by appointment Mon-Fri 0900-1700, £3.50.*

To the north of here is the village of **Haroldswick**, home of Britain's most northerly post office, where your postcards are sent with a special stamp to inform everyone of this fact. Here you'll also find **Unst Boat Haven** ① *T01957-711528, May-Sep daily 1100-1700, £2, children free,* where you can see a beautifully presented collection of traditional boats and fishing artefacts. A little way further north is the **Unst Heritage Centre** ① *May-Sep daily 1100-1700,* which has a museum of local history and island life. Nearby is an RAF radar-tracking station at Saxa Vord. The road ends at Skaw, where there's a lovely beach and Britain's most northerly house. The road northwest from Haroldswick leads to the head of **Burra Firth**, a sea inlet flanked by high cliffs, and site of Britain's most northerly golf course.

To the west of Burra Firth is the remote **Hermaness National Nature Reserve**, 2422 acres of dramatic coastal scenery and wild moorland that is home to over 100,000 nesting seabirds, including gannets and the largest number of puffins and great skuas (or 'bonxies') in Shetland. There's an excellent **visitor centre** ① *T01975-711278, mid-Apr to mid-Sep daily 0800-1700,* in the former lighthouse keeper's shore station, where you can pick up a leaflet which shows the marked route into the reserve, and see the artistic efforts of many of Unst's children. Whilst in the reserve, make sure you keep to the marked paths to avoid being attacked by bonxies; they are highly protective and they will attack if they think that their territory is being threatened.

The views from Hermaness are wonderful, out to the offshore stacks and skerries including **Muckle Flugga**, and then to the wide open North Atlantic Ocean. Muckle Flugga is the site of the most northerly lighthouse in Britain, built in 1857-1858 by Thomas Stevenson, father of Robert Louis Stevenson. The writer visited the island in 1869, and the illustrated map in his novel *Treasure Island* bears a striking similarity to the outline of Unst. Beyond the lighthouse is **Out Stack**, which marks the most northerly point on the British Isles. With nothing between you and the North Pole but water, this is the place to sit and contemplate what it feels like to be at the end of the world.

Shetland listings

For hotel and restaurant price codes and other relevant information, see pages 13-19.

● Where to stay

Lerwick and around *p65, map p66*
Most of Shetland's best accommodation is outside Lerwick, where hotels are mostly geared towards the oil industry. During the peak months of Jul-Aug and the Folk Festival in Apr, it's a good idea to book in advance. There are several decent

guesthouses and B&Bs in town, which are all much of a muchness. The tourist office can supply details.

£££ Kveldsro House Hotel, Greenfield Pl, T01595-692195, www.shetlandhotels. com. The most luxurious hotel in town. Pronounced 'kel-ro', it overlooks the harbour and has an upmarket restaurant (**£££**) as well as cheaper bar food.

£££ Westhall B&B, Lower Sound, T01595-690364, www.bedandbreakfastlerwick.co.uk. A big old house, just 20 mins' walk from the centre along the bay. 3 rooms en suite. They also offer a cottage from £100 per night for 2, or £120 for 4, min 3 nights. Recommended.

£££-££ Brentham House, 7 Harbour St, T01950-460201, www.brenthamhouse.com. 3 en suite rooms and 1 suite (**£££**). Luxurious rooms featuring Victorian bathtubs and with a continental breakfast waiting in the fridge.

££ Glen Orchy House, 20 Knab Rd, T01595-692031, www.guesthouselerwick.com. Excellent guest house with 23 en suite rooms and its own Thai restaurant.

£ SYHA hostel, Islesburgh House, King Harald St, T01595-692114, www.islesburgh. org.uk. Open Apr-Sep. Clean and well-run with 64 beds, with an excellent café.

Camping

Clickimin Caravan & Camp Site, near Clickimin Leisure Centre and loch on the western edge of the town, T01595-741000, www.srt.org.uk. May-Sep. £5.80-£12 for a pitch.

Central Mainland *p68*

£££ Herrislea House Hotel, Tingwall, near the airport, by the crossroads, T01595-840208, www.herrisleahouse.co.uk. 13 en suite rooms. Country house in lovely setting with well-furnished rooms. Their Phoenix restaurant (**£££**) specializes in local meat (Mon-Sat 1830-2045), the **Starboard Tack** bar has live music.

££ Hildasay Guest House, Scalloway, in the upper part of the village, T01595-880822. Has disabled facilities and arranges fishing trips.

££ Scalloway Hotel, Main St, Scalloway, a few miles west of Lerwick, T01595-880444, www.scallowayhotel.com. A comfortable, modest hotel with a growing reputation for serving up the best seafood and hearty steak pie dinners (**££-£**) for miles around.

££ The Westings Inn, Wormadale, near Tingwall, T01595-840242, www.originart. com/westings. 6 rooms. Whilst it wins no prizes for decor, you'll be well looked

after at this B&B with views over Whiteness Voe. Decent bar food and real ales, also has a campsite.

The Westside *p69*

£££ Burrastow House, 2 miles southwest of Walls, T01595-809307 www.burrastow house.co.uk. Open Apr-Nov. 6 rooms. A restored 18th-century house overlooking Vaila Sound, it's full of character. The owner cooks magnificent seafood, see Restaurants, below. **££££** including dinner. Children half price, under 3s free. Recommended.

££ Pomona, Gruting, east of Brig o' Waas, T01595-810438. Friendly and comfortable, modern bungalow. An excellent base for seal, otter and birdwatching. 4 miles from Walls, where there's a shop and petrol station.

££ Skeoverick, a mile or so north of Walls, T01595-809349. A welcoming B&B with 4 rooms. The owners allow guests to use the kitchen to prepare meals.

Camping

Voe House, Walls, www.camping-bods.com. This is a camping *böd* – a restored 18th-century house overlooking the village. Apr-Sep. Book through Lerwick tourist office.

Foula *p69*

££ Leraback, Foula, T01595-753226, www. originart.com/leraback/leraback. Modern crofthouse bungalow with three bedrooms. 3-course dinner included in the price (served at 1815) and self-catering also available. Free collection from, and drop off at, the pier.

Self-catering

There is self-catering accommodation available on Foula in a cottage sleeping 4-6 people. Contact Mr R Holbourn, T01595-753232.

Papa Stour *p70*

£ Hurdiback Hostel, T01595-873227, www.hurdibackhostel.co.uk. Small, secluded hostel with 2 rooms of 4 bunks. You can order bread and eggs before you arrive.

South Mainland p70

There's accommodation in Bigton, Scousburgh and around Sumburgh, but it is limited.

££ Setterbrae, Scousburgh, T1950-460468, www.setterbrae.co.uk. 3 rooms overlooking the Loch of Spiggie.

££ The Spiggie Hotel, Scousburgh, Dunrossness, T01950-460409, www.thespiggiehotel.co.uk. Less than 30 mins' drive from Lerwick and close to Sumburgh airport. A small, family-run hotel with 6 rooms, overlooking Spiggie Loch, with a cosy bar (think postage stamp size) serving good real ales and tasty seafood. Also sells permits for fishing.

££ Sumburgh Hotel, next to Jarlshof, Sumburgh, T01950-460201, www.sumburgh hotel.com. 32 en suite rooms. 19th-century former home of Laird of Sumburgh, with great views across to Fair Isle and 2 bars and a good restaurant (**££**).

££-£ Hayhoull, Bigton T01950-422206, www.bedandbreakfastshetland.com. This spick and span B&B has 3 rooms with beautiful views of St Ninian's Isle and towards Foula, Evening meals are available. Recommended.

Camping
Betty Mouat's Cottage, next to the excavations at Old Scatness and the airport, is this camping *böd*. It sleeps up to 8 and is open Apr-Sep. Book through Lerwick tourist office.

Fair Isle p72
There are a few places to stay on the island, but accommodation must be booked in advance and includes meals. There are no hotels, pubs or restaurants.

£££ Fair Isle Lodge and Bird Observatory, T01595-760258, www.fairislebirdobs.co.uk. The price is for full-board accommodation in private rooms. No B&B available.

££ South Lighthouse, T01595-760355, www.southlightfairisle.co.uk. Stunning location, the price includes dinner and a packed lunch.

££ Upper Leogh www.kathycoull.com, T01595-760248. Situated beside a working crofthouse, with sea views. Offers full board and is run by Kathy Coull.

Self-catering
Self-catering cottage, T01595-760225. Available at Springfield Croft House.

North Mainland p73
£££ Busta House Hotel, Brae, T01806-522506, www.bustahouse.com. Open all year. 20 rooms. The best place to stay around Brae and probably one of the best on Shetland is this luxurious and wonderfully atmospheric 16th-century country house overlooking Busta Voe about 1½ miles from Brae village. The superb restaurant (**£££**) is one of the finest on Shetland, with a selection of malts to match, and there are also meals in the bar. Recommended.

££ Almara, Upper Urafirth, T01806-503261, www.almara.shetland.co.uk. This friendly and comfortable B&B is the pick of the bunch.

££ Westayre, Westayre, Muckle Roe, Brae, T01806-522368, www.westayre.shetland. co.uk. A working croft.

Camping
Johnny Notion's Camping Böd, in Hamnavoe, Northmavine, www.camping-bods.com, reached by a side road which branches north from the road between Hillswick and Eshaness. This is the birth-place of John Williamson, an 18th-century craftsman who developed an effective innoculation against smallpox. Apr-Sep, has no electricity. Book through Lerwick tourist office.

Sail Loft, in Voe by the pier. Apr-Sep. This former fishing store is now Shetland's largest camping *böd*.

Whalsay and Out Skerries p74
Hugh Mc Diarmid's Camping Böd (The Grieve House), near Symbister, www.camping-bods.com. Apr-Sep. The former home of this great poet, see page 74. No electricity.

A böd for the night

There is only one youth hostel in Shetland, but budget travellers shouldn't panic. **Shetland Camping Böd** project has developed a network of camping *böds* (pronounced 'burd') which provide basic and cheap digs throughout the islands.

A *böd* was a building used to house fishermen and their gear during the fishing season and the name has been used to describe these types of accommodation which are similar to English 'camping barns'. They are all located in scenic places and each has its own fascinating history. They are very basic and the more remote ones have no electricity. You'll need to bring a stove, cooking and eating utensils, a sleeping bag and a torch (flashlight). All *böds* must be booked in advance through the TIC in Lerwick and cost £6 per person per night without electricity, or £8 per person per night with electricity. They are open from April till the end of September. There are at present nine camping *böds* on Shetland (listed in the relevant places). See also www.camping-bods.com.

Yell *p74*

££ Norwind B&B, Mid Yell, T01957-702312. Offers 2 double and twin rooms (all en suite) in a comfortable, modern bungalow. Evening meal and a packed lunch can be booked in advance. 15 mins from the ferry.
££ Pinewood Guest House, South Aywick, between Burravoe and Mid Yell, T01975-702427.
££ Post Office, Gutcher, T01957-744201. Friendly and welcoming.

Camping

Windhouse Lodge www.camping-bods.com. Apr-Sep. A well-equipped camping *böd* below the ruins of haunted Windhouse.

Fetlar *p75*

££ The Gord, Houbie, T01975-733227. B&B attached to the shop in Houbie. 3 en suite rooms, offers dinner and is easy to find.

Camping

£ The Garths Campsite, Fetlar, T01975-733227. May-Sep. Overlooks the beach at Tresta and has good facilities. Pitch up for £7.

Unst *p75*

There's a decent selection of accommodation on Unst.

£££ Buness House, T01975-711315. Top choice has to be the faded grandeur of this 17th-century Haa in Baltasound which has fine views. Staying here is a bizarre and rather surreal experience, given that you are on the most northerly island in Britain. The house is crammed full of Indian Raj relics, and the stuffed eagle, tiger and leopard skins hanging in the hallway are a wildlife close up almost as impressive, though considerably more unsettling and un-'PC', as the Hermaness Nature Reserve in the north of the island that the family own. The food is excellent (**£££**) and accommodation comfortable.
££ Baltasound Hotel, T01957-711334, www.baltasound-hotel.shetland.co.uk. Wooden chalets and a small but well-stocked bar serving decent food.
££ Gerratoun, Haroldswick, T01975-711323. Claims to be Britain's most northerly B&B. Located within walking distance of Hermaness and with excellent views, this restored crofthouse offers 1 twin bedroom. Caters for special diets.
£ Gardiesfauld Hostel, Baltasound, T01975-755259, www.gardiesfauld.shetland.co.uk. Apr-Sep. An independent hostel, which also hires bikes.
£ Prestegaard, T01975-755234. A Victorian house at Uyeasound on the south coast near the ferry. Terrific sea views.

🍴 Restaurants

Despite a ready supply of fresh local produce, with a few notable exceptions (and of course during its excellent 'Flavour of Shetland' food festival in Jun), the archipelago can feel like a gastronomic desert. The hotels and guesthouses listed above under Where to stay are far and away the best options, especially **Burrastow House** and **Busta House Hotel.**

Lerwick and around *p65, map p66*

£££ Monty's Bistro & Deli, 5 Mounthooly St, T01595-696655. Tue-Sat. Directly across from the Lounge (see bars below), this is the best place to eat in Lerwick. It offers good modern Scottish cooking, including huge thick-cut halibut steaks and a selection of fine wines in a cosy, informal setting.

£££-££ Hay's Dock, Shetland Museum, www.haysdock.co.uk, see Places in Lerwick, page 66. This café/restaurant is worth a try – as is their salt beef Shetland bannock – but just like Monty's their main dishes are a little pricey.

££ Brasserie Restaurant, Lerwick Hotel, 15 South Rd. For dinner or bar lunch. Its carvery is a roast dinner lover's dream, with seaweed-fed Shetland lamb served with Shetland Black potatoes. Recommended.

££ Gallery Restaurant, Kveldsro Hotel, see Where to stay, above. Offers the chance to watch the boats sail by as you eat. Pan-fried scallops, crab and Shetland lamb pâté, and a traditional roast menu on Sun.

£ Osla's Café Bar & Bistro, 88 Commercial St, T01595-696005. Mon-Sat until 2000, Sun 1200-1700. Bustling café serving a wide range of coffees, pancakes and other snacks, and boasting the islands' only beer garden.

£ Peerie Shop Café, Esplanade, T01595-692816. Mon-Sat 0900-1800. The best cappuccino in Shetland and muffins the size of Bressay. Also does cheering soups.

Central Mainland *p68*

£ Castle Café, New Rd, Scalloway, near the castle, T01595-880270. Damn fine chippy serving takeaway or sit-in fish and chips.

£ Da Haaf Restaurant, NAFC Marine Centre, Porth Arthur, Scalloway, T01595-772480, www.nafc.ac.uk. Mon-Fri 0830-1600. A canteen-style restaurant in the North Atlantic Fisheries college specializing in seafood. Does a good fish supper, as well as a more upmarket menu for the evenings.

The Westside *p69*

£££ Burrastow House, see Where to stay, above. Open to non-residents Sat-Sun. The Belgian owner of this restored 18th-century house cooks magnificent seafood. This is the best place to eat on the islands, so you'll need to book ahead. Recommended.

North Mainland *p73*

£££ Busta House Hotel, Brae, see Where to stay, above. The best option hereabouts, serving Shetland hill lamb, free range pork from Unst and Yell Sound scallops. Has a good malt whisky selection.

££ Frankies Fish and Chips, Brae, T01806-522700. Serves all sort of fried seafood (squid, skate wings, prawns) as well as the old classics. They also steam the fattest juiciest local mussels for those watching their waistlines.

££-£ Pierhead Restaurant and Bar, Voe, T01806-588332. Serves decent meals: locally caught fish and shellfish are the mainstays of the menu. And in the evenings, Shetland's young fiddle players play for pints.

£ Da Bod Café, Hillswick, T01806-503348. Thu-Sun 1200-1800. Shetland's oldest pub, now converted into a vegetarian café serving light bites and snacks. Café also hosts live music and storytelling events.

Yell *p74*

£ Old Haa Museum Café, Burravoe, south-east Yell. Open 1000-1600. A small café on the ground floor of the museum. Serves teas, coffees, great home-baking and sandwiches.

£ Wind Dog Café, opposite the Post Office, Gutcher, T01957-744321, www.winddogcafe.co.uk. Mon-Fri 0900-1700, Sat-Sun 1000-1700. Evening meals are served from 1830. Internet access in cosy surroundings, where you can enjoy home-baking, coffee, soup of the day or a burger, or even browse their small library. Welcoming and recommended.

Unst *p75*
£££-££ Baltasound Hotel, T01975-711334. Serves meals and drinks to non-residents.

🎵 Bars and clubs

Lerwick and around *p65, map p66*
Lounge, Mounthooly St, near the TIC. The locals mingle downstairs, whilst upstairs the bar is quite touristy but definitely one of the best places for a drink. Moreover, this remains a magnet for enjoying planned and impromptu sessions of Shetland's wonderful fiddle and folk music. Whenever you arrive, there's usually someone playing.

✺ Festivals

Lerwick and around *p65, map p66*
The *Shetland Times*, www.shetlandtimes.co.uk, has details what is going on. Also check the tourist board's website, www.visitshetland.com, or ring T08701-999440.
Jan Up-Helly-Aa, www.uphellyaa.org. Lerwick's annual fire festival is celebrated on the last Tue in Jan with torch-lit processions, Viking costumes and the burning of a Viking longboat. If you miss this one, there are a number across the islands over the next 2 months. See also page 67.
May Shetland Folk Festival, www.shetlandfolkfestival.com. Folk music has a strong following in Shetland and this is one of Scotland's top folk events. Over 3 days in early May musicians from around the globe come to play.

Jun Shetland Food Festival, www.visitshetland.com. The 4-day 'Flavour of Shetland' food festival is a gastronome's dream with the best of Shetland lamb and shellfish among the treats to be found by the harbour in Lerwick. It's a major festival with dozens of boats sailing across from Norway to enjoy the festivities, so if you fancy a mid-summer party you know where to come.
Mid-Oct Shetland Accordion and Fiddle Festival, for details of both events contact the Folk Festival office, 5 Burns Lane, Lerwick, T01595-693162 or www.shetandaccordionandfiddle.com.

◯ Shopping

Lerwick and around *p65, map p66*
Ninian, 110 Commercial St, T01595-696655 For new takes on traditional Fair Isle knitting.
Peerie Shop, Esplanade T01595-692816 Colourful homeware, postcards and knits.
Shetland Times, Commerical St, T01595-695531. For books about Shetland.
The Spiders Web, 51 Commercial St, T01595-695246. Mon-Sat 0900-1700. The place to buy authentic Shetland knit-wear sourced directly from the local knitters. Hand-spun yarn and hand-knitted Fair Isle jumpers, waistcoats, cardigans, scarves and shawls.

Central Mainland *p68*
Shetland Woollen Company, next to Scalloway Castle. Where you can buy the famous Shetland wool and Fair Isle jumpers.

The Westside *p69*
Shetland Jewellery, Soundside, Weisdale, T01595-830275, www.shetlandjewellery.com. Mon-Fri 0900-1700, Jun-Aug also Sat 1000-1700 and Sun 1400-1700. This small workshop and studio is set right beside a sea loch. Great place to buy authentic gold and silver Shetland rings and brooches, etc. Guided tours available over a cup of tea.

⚙ What to do

Shetland *p63, map p64*
Boat trips

A boat trip to the seabird colonies on Noss and Bressay is unmissable, so don't even think about coming here and not doing it. **Seabirds-and-seals**, Bressay, T07831-217042 or T07876-550224, www.seabirds-and-seals.com. Award-winning wildlife cruises run by Jonathan Wills. If you go at the right time of year, you are almost guaranteed to see seals, porpoises and the astounding gannetry on the spectacular cliffs of Noss' east coast. Trips leave at 1000 and 1400 mid-Apr to mid-Sep, weather permitting, £45, concessions £40, student £30, under 16s £25, under 5s free.

If you want to learn about the Islands' stunning geology and how man and nature has made these Islands their own Allen Fraser of **Geo-Tours**, Burra Isle, T01595-859218, www.shetlandgeology.com, has a fine grasp of the last 500 million years. **Mousa Boat Trips**, Sandwick, T01950-431367, www.mousa.co.uk. Runs daily trips Apr-Sep to Mousa from Sandsayre aboard *M/V Solan IV*. Departs Mon, Tue, Thu-Sat 1300, Wed 1000, Sun 1330, allowing 3 hrs on the island. The 15-min crossing provides the chance to spot seals and seabirds before exploring well preserved Pictish brochs on Mousa. £16, concessions £14, children £7. Trip also suitable for wheelchairs. Evening trips to see the storm petrels also available from mid-May.

Photography

Island Trails, Bigton, T07880-950228, www.island-trails.co.uk. A variety of guides tours by James Tait. Prices vary, guided half-day walk of St Ninian's Isle £20 pp.

Sea kayaking

Sea Kayak Shetland, T01592-840272, www.seakayakshetland.co.uk. Tours with Angus Nichol. Full day trip £75 pp, introductory session £25.

Tour operators

John Leask & Son, the Esplanade, Lerwick, T01595-693162, www.leaskstravel.co.uk. Travel agent and tour operator. Can arrange fly-drive packages to Shetland with car hire and accommodation. Also offer a variety of bus tours, prices depending on the destination.

⊖ Transport

Lerwick and around *p65, map p66*
For more information, see Getting there, page 66.
Bus Bus No 4 runs to **Scalloway** (Mon-Sat) and there are also buses to **Walls** (No 9); **Sandness, Aith** (No 9 and 12); **North Roe** (No 21); **Hillswick** (No 21); **Vidlin** (No19); **Toft** (No 23), 1 hr; **Mossbank** (No 23). All buses leave from Lerwick's Viking bus station. There are several buses daily between **Lerwick**, **Sandwick** and **Sumburgh Airport**. 2 buses daily Mon-Sat to **Quendale**, with a change at **Channerwick junction**. Regular daily buses from **Lerwick** stop at the Sumburgh Hotel, **Scatness** and **Grutness Pier** (for Fair Isle) en route to the airport.

Regular buses Mon-Sat to **Brae** and **Hillswick** to the northwest, and **Toft** and **Mossbank** to the north, pass through **Voe**. To **Hillswick** and **Toft/Mossbank** stop in **Brae**. There is a daily bus service from here to **Hillswick**, Mon-Sat, 1710. From there, a feeder service (No 21) continues to **Eshaness**, 20 mins. Contact **Johnson Transport**, T01806-522331. There are daily buses to **Laxo** and **Vidlin**, run by **Whites Coaches**, T01595-809443.

For detailed information on all bus services, T01595-744868, or see www.zettrans.org.uk.

Car hire Bolts Car Hire, Toll Clock Shopping Centre, 26 North Rd, T01595-693636, www.boltscarhire.co.uk. John Leask & Son, the Esplanade, T01595-693162, www.leaskstravel.co.uk; Star Rent-a-Car, 22 Commercial Rd, T01595-692075, www.starrentacar.co.uk, which also has an office at Sumburgh Airport.

Cycle hire Grantfield Garage, North Rd, T01595-692709, www.grantfieldgarage. co.uk. Mon-Sat 0800-2300, Sun 1100-2300. Hires bikes for £5 per day or £30 per week.

Ferry Ferry links with the UK are provided mostly by **Northlink Ferries**, T0845-600 0449, www.northlinkferries.co.uk. They operate car ferries from Lerwick to **Aberdeen**. A single fare for a passenger seat costs £40.50 in peak season (return fare is double). A car costs £144 single. A 2-berth cabin costs up to £137 for a 'Premium' berth in high season. Children aged 4-16 half price and under 4s free.

There are regular daily car ferries between Lerwick and **Bressay**, £5 per passenger, £12.50 per car return, 5 mins.

To **Skerries**, Tue and Thu, 2½ hrs, £5 per passenger, £6.50 per car one-way, T01806-244200. To **Fair Isle** alternate Thu, 4½ hrs, £5 per passenger, £24 per car one way.

Taxi There are several taxi companies in Lerwick: **6050 Cabs**, T01595-696050; **Abbys Taxis**, T01595-696666; **Allied Taxis**, T01595-690069; **Sinclairs Taxis**, T01595-694617.

Bressay p67
Ferry Noss can only be visited from late May-late Aug Tue, Wed and Fri-Sun, 1000-1700. From the 'Wait here' sign overlooking Noss sound on the east side of Bressay an inflatable dinghy shuttles back and forth to Noss during the island's opening hours. In bad weather, call the tourist office, T01595-693434, to check if it's sailing. A **postcar** service runs once a day Mon-Sat from Maryfield ferry terminal to Noss Sound, T01595-820200.

Central Mainland p68
Air Tingwall airport, T01595-840246, has flights to most of the smaller islands, including

the **Skerries**, and getting to the airport is straightforward, as the regular buses between Lerwick and Westside stop in Tingwall.

Bus There are buses Mon-Sat between **Scalloway and Lerwick**, John Leask & Son, see What to do, page 82.

The Westside p69
Bus A minibus (No 10 and No 11) runs to **Sandness** from **Walls** once a day Mon-Sat. Contact A&K Transport, T01595-809337.

Ferry There's a passenger/cargo ferry service between **West Mainland** and **Papa Stour**, £5 per passenger, £6.50 per car one way, Mon, Wed, Fri, Sat and Sun, 40 mins. Ferries should be booked through Shetland Council, T01595-745804. There are ferries from Walls to **Foula** with BK Marine on Tue and Thu year round and also Sat in summer, T01595-743976, www.bkmarine.co.uk.

South Mainland p70
Air Flybe, www.flybe.com, flies directly (using **Loganair**, T01595-840246) from Sumburgh to **Aberdeen**, **Kirkwall**, **Inverness**, **Glasgow** and **Edinburgh**. The airline also connects with **Bergen** in Norway in the summer. **Loganair** also operates a regular service from Sumburgh to **Fair Isle**.

Ferry Regular daily car ferries from **Scalloway** to **Foula**, alternate Thu, 3 hrs, £5 per passenger, £24 per car one way; and **South Mainland** to **Fair Isle**, Tue, Sat and alternate Thu, 2½ hrs, £5 per passenger, £24 per car.

North Mainland p73
Ferry There are frequent car and passenger ferries from **Toft** on North Mainland to **Ulsta** on the south coast of **Yell**. It's not essential, but it's a good idea to book in advance, T01595-745804, £5 per passenger, £12.50 per car return, 20 mins.

Whalsay and Out Skerries *p74*

Ferry There's a less frequent car ferry service between **East Mainland** and **Skerries**, Mon, Fri, Sat and Sun, 1½ hrs, £5 per passenger, £6.50 per car one way. There are regular daily car and passenger ferries between **Laxo** and **Symbister**. To book, call T01806-566259. There are ferries to the Skerries from **Vidlin**, about 3 miles northeast of Laxo. For bookings, call **Shetland Council**, T01595-745805.

Yell *p74*

Ferry There are regular daily car ferries to **Belmont** on **Unst**, 10 mins, and **Fetlar**, 25 mins, from **Gutcher**, £5 per passenger and £12.50 per car return. Booking is advised, T01595-745804.

Fetlar *p75*

Bus There's a post car service which runs around Fetlar from the ferry once a day on Mon, Wed and Fri, T01975-733227.

Ferry There are regular car and passenger ferries between **Oddsta** in the northwest of Fetlar, **Gutcher** (Yell) and **Belmont** (Unst).

Unst *p75*

Bus There's an island bus service, which runs a few times a day, Mon-Sat between **Baltasound**, **Belmont** and **Haroldswick**, P&T Coaches, T01975-711666.

ⓘ Directory

Lerwick and around *p65, map p66*
Banks Bank of Scotland, Clydesdale and **Royal** are on Commercial St. **Lloyds** TSB is on the Esplanade. **Embassies and consulates** Denmark, Iceland and **Netherlands**, Hay & Company, 66 Commercial Rd, T01595-692533; **Finland**, France, Germany and **Norway**, Shearer Shipping Services, Garthspool, T01595-692556; **Sweden**, Iain Tulloch, Linnabretta, 13 Stout's Court, Lerwick T01595-692991. **Laundry** Lerwick Laundry, 36 Market St, T01595-693043, Mon-Sat, service washes only. **Medical services** Gilbert Bain Hospital, South Rd, T01595-743000; Lerwick Health Centre, opposite Gilbert Bain Hospital, T01595-693201. **Post** 46 Commercial St, Mon-Fri 0900-1700, Sat 0900-1230; Toll Clock Shopping Centre, 26 North Rd, T01595-695362.

Contents

Footnotes

Index

Titles available in the Footprint *Focus* range

Latin America	UK RRP	US RRP
Bahia & Salvador	£7.99	$11.95
Brazilian Amazon	£7.99	$11.95
Brazilian Pantanal	£6.99	$9.95
Buenos Aires & Pampas	£7.99	$11.95
Cartagena & Caribbean Coast	£7.99	$11.95
Costa Rica	£8.99	$12.95
Cuzco, La Paz & Lake Titicaca	£8.99	$12.95
El Salvador	£5.99	$8.95
Guadalajara & Pacific Coast	£6.99	$9.95
Guatemala	£8.99	$12.95
Guyana, Guyane & Suriname	£5.99	$8.95
Havana	£6.99	$9.95
Honduras	£7.99	$11.95
Nicaragua	£7.99	$11.95
Northeast Argentina & Uruguay	£8.99	$12.95
Paraguay	£5.99	$8.95
Quito & Galápagos Islands	£7.99	$11.95
Recife & Northeast Brazil	£7.99	$11.95
Rio de Janeiro	£8.99	$12.95
São Paulo	£5.99	$8.95
Uruguay	£6.99	$9.95
Venezuela	£8.99	$12.95
Yucatán Peninsula	£6.99	$9.95

Asia	UK RRP	US RRP
Angkor Wat	£5.99	$8.95
Bali & Lombok	£8.99	$12.95
Chennai & Tamil Nadu	£8.99	$12.95
Chiang Mai & Northern Thailand	£7.99	$11.95
Goa	£6.99	$9.95
Gulf of Thailand	£8.99	$12.95
Hanoi & Northern Vietnam	£8.99	$12.95
Ho Chi Minh City & Mekong Delta	£7.99	$11.95
Java	£7.99	$11.95
Kerala	£7.99	$11.95
Kolkata & West Bengal	£5.99	$8.95
Mumbai & Gujarat	£8.99	$12.95

Africa & Middle East	UK RRP	US RRP
Beirut	£6.99	$9.95
Cairo & Nile Delta	£8.99	$12.95
Damascus	£5.99	$8.95
Durban & KwaZulu Natal	£8.99	$12.95
Fès & Northern Morocco	£8.99	$12.95
Jerusalem	£8.99	$12.95
Johannesburg & Kruger National Park	£7.99	$11.95
Kenya's Beaches	£8.99	$12.95
Kilimanjaro & Northern Tanzania	£8.99	$12.95
Luxor to Aswan	£8.99	$12.95
Nairobi & Rift Valley	£7.99	$11.95
Red Sea & Sinai	£7.99	$11.95
Zanzibar & Pemba	£7.99	$11.95

Europe	UK RRP	US RRP
Bilbao & Basque Region	£6.99	$9.95
Brittany West Coast	£7.99	$11.95
Cádiz & Costa de la Luz	£6.99	$9.95
Granada & Sierra Nevada	£6.99	$9.95
Languedoc: Carcassonne to Montpellier	£7.99	$11.95
Málaga	£5.99	$8.95
Marseille & Western Provence	£7.99	$11.95
Orkney & Shetland Islands	£5.99	$8.95
Santander & Picos de Europa	£7.99	$11.95
Sardinia: Alghero & the North	£7.99	$11.95
Sardinia: Cagliari & the South	£7.99	$11.95
Seville	£5.99	$8.95
Sicily: Palermo & the Northwest	£7.99	$11.95
Sicily: Catania & the Southeast	£7.99	$11.95
Siena & Southern Tuscany	£7.99	$11.95
Sorrento, Capri & Amalfi Coast	£6.99	$9.95
Skye & Outer Hebrides	£6.99	$9.95
Verona & Lake Garda	£7.99	$11.95

North America	UK RRP	US RRP
Vancouver & Rockies	£8.99	$12.95

Australasia	UK RRP	US RRP
Brisbane & Queensland	£8.99	$12.95
Perth	£7.99	$11.95

For the latest books, e-books and a wealth of travel information, visit us at:
www.footprinttravelguides.com.

Join us on facebook for the latest travel news, product releases, offers and amazing competitions:
www.facebook.com/footprintbooks.